STORY OF
JOHN WAYNE

CONTRIBUTORS:
JOEL MCIVER, NEIL CROSSLEY, SCOTT REEVES

FOX CHAPEL
PUBLISHING

Used under license. All rights reserved. This version published by Fox Chapel Publishing Company, Inc., 903 Square Street, Mount Joy, PA 17552.

For more information about the Future plc group, go to http://www.futureplc.com.

ISBN 978-1-4971-0435-8

Library of Congress Control Number: 2023952724

To learn more about the other great books from Fox Chapel Publishing, or to find a retailer near you, call toll-free 800-457-9112 or visit us at *www.FoxChapelPublishing.com*.

We are always looking for talented authors. To submit an idea, please send a brief inquiry to acquisitions@foxchapelpublishing.com.

Printed in Malaysia
First printing

"COURAGE IS BEING SCARED TO DEATH, BUT SADDLING UP ANYWAY.

★ John Wayne

When you're a boy named Marion growing up in the state of Iowa, you toughen up fast. Yet few boys go from riding a horse to school to sitting astride a galloping steed on the set of a big-budget blockbuster movie that will be seen across the globe. Marion Robert Morrison did, and he achieved global stardom with nothing more than grit, determination, and no small amount of hard work and bravery.

In time, he would come to be known as John Wayne, one of the most iconic titles in the history of cinema. This is the story of how he rose from a quiet rural upbringing to become a Hollywood hero and the most famous cowboy the big screen has ever seen. From his early days lugging props around movie sets to his first big break, early flops, and biggest hits; to the women who won his heart (however briefly), his pioneering methods, and his legacy today. This is the tale of the man who made the Western his own, spoke as he found, and above all, embodied what it was to be an American patriot in a world of ever-changing fortunes. This is the story of John Wayne.

CONTENTS

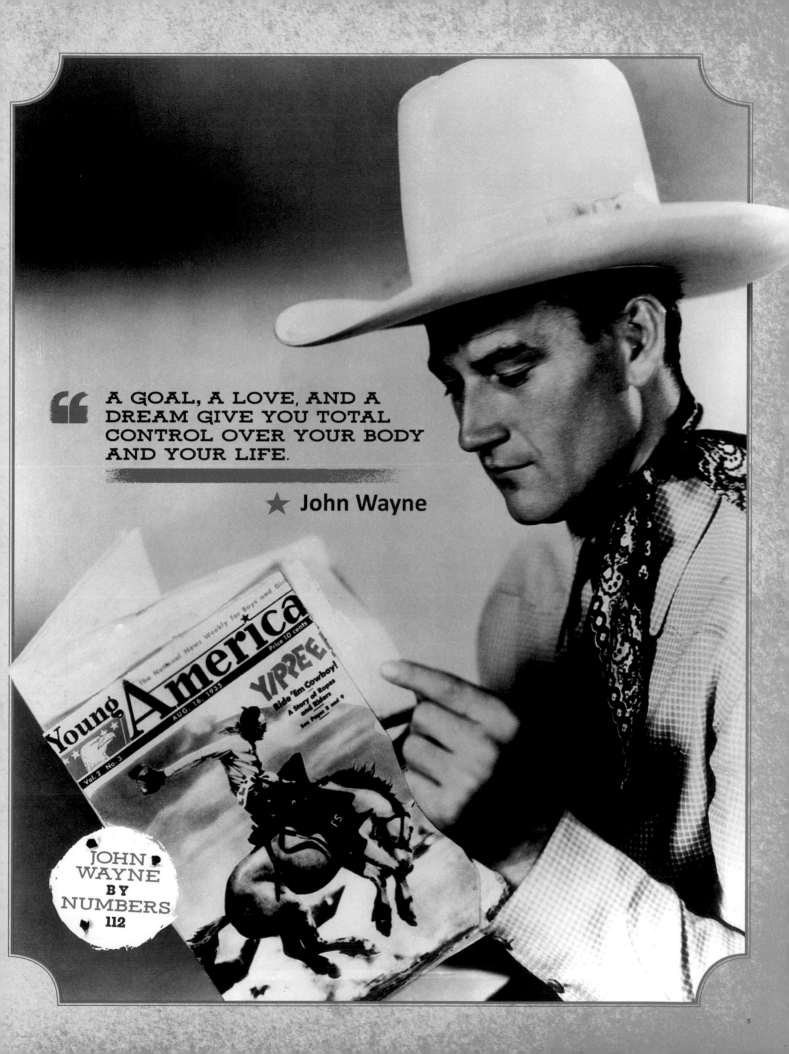

> " A GOAL, A LOVE, AND A DREAM GIVE YOU TOTAL CONTROL OVER YOUR BODY AND YOUR LIFE.

★ John Wayne

JOHN WAYNE BY NUMBERS 112

CHAPTER 1

★

THE NAME'S DUKE

EARLY
YEARS

How a Midwestern boy named Marion distinguished
himself thanks to physical prowess and sheer
determination.

The house that Wayne was born in.

Wayne (left) with his father Leonard and brother Robert.

Wayne's hometown of Winterset, Iowa, is known for its covered bridges.

For the 30,000 people a year who visit the house where John Wayne was born, it must be difficult to envisage how such a gargantuan star can have emerged from such a modest dwelling. The tiny white clapboard house is situated in the small town of Winterset, Iowa, 35 miles southwest of the state capital, Des Moines. Wayne lived there for only three years, but it is now the only museum in the world dedicated to him.

These days, the house is crammed with period-era furniture and memorabilia from Wayne's career, including an eye patch he wore in the original *True Grit* and an autographed copy of a 1972 biography entitled *The John Wayne Story*.

A dim, back corner room, measuring just eight feet wide and 15 feet long, is where the infant Wayne drew his first breath, and it's a space that instills a reverential hush among the steady stream of visitors.

 HE TOOK THE FAMILY WEST TO SOUTHERN CALIFORNIA WHERE THEY TRIED RANCHING IN THE MOJAVE DESERT.

Had his family remained in this sleepy Midwestern town, it seems unlikely that he would have risen to prominence in the way that he did. But a move west and a series of chance events set him on a path that would secure his reputation as one of the greatest movie icons of all time.

Wayne was born Marion Robert Morrison on May 26, 1907, to Mary Alberta "Molly" Brown and Clyde Leonard Morrison, a pharmacist. He was of English, Ulster-Scots, and Irish ancestry, the Morrisons originally hailing from the Isle of Lewis in the Outer Hebrides. When Clyde developed a lung condition, he decided to move to warmer climes in an effort to improve his health. He took the family west to southern California, where they tried ranching in the Mojave Desert. So began a whole new way of life for Wayne and his younger brother, Robert, his only sibling. They rode a horse to school and would swim in a local irrigation ditch.

In 1916, when Wayne was seven, the family moved again, this time to Lancaster,

Images Alamy

9

A view of Moyse Field on the campus of Glendale Union High School (now called Glendale High School).

California. A few years later they moved for a third time when Clyde's attempts to become a farmer eventually failed.

The family settled in Glendale, California, where Clyde ran a drug store. By his mid-teens, Wayne was rising at four every morning to deliver newspapers, and after playing football he would make deliveries for his father and other local stores in the evenings.

It was while living in Glendale that Wayne received his famous nickname "Duke." This was the name of the family's Airedale Terrier, and the young Wayne spent so much time with the animal that he earned the nickname "Little Duke." He far preferred it to Marion and the name stuck.

Wayne attended Glendale Union High School and excelled at both sport and academic study. He became part of the school's football team and its 1924 league championship-winning squad. He also joined its debate team, contributed to the school newspaper's sports column, and took part in numerous theatrical productions.

Towards the end of Wayne's high school years, two setbacks occurred that would transform his career plans. The first came when he applied to the US Naval Academy in Annapolis but narrowly failed admission due to insufficient grades. Instead, in 1925, he went to the University of Southern California (USC) on a football scholarship and majored in pre-law.

Wayne played college football at the University of Southern California (circa 1927).

BELOW
An aerial view of the Westwood campus at USC, California.

10

UNITED STATES
NAVAL ACADEMY
FOUNDED 1845

An Airedale
Terrier like Wayne's
beloved Duke.

By the age of 18, Wayne was an imposing 6 foot 4 inches tall and playing on the USC football team under revered coach Howard Jones. But in 1927, after two years at USC, a second setback occurred that prompted a major change in his fortunes.

Like many of his peers, Wayne was an avid surfer and would take any available opportunity to get out on his board at Newport Beach. During one surfing session Wayne was knocked off his board by a wave and forced underwater, which left him with a broken collarbone.

Years later, Wayne admitted that he was too terrified of coach Howard Jones to reveal the actual cause of his injury. He attempted to bluff his way through football practices, but the injury was too painful. He was dropped from the team and lost his athletic scholarship.

Without the scholarship, he had to pay for boarding and tuition fees, something he was unable to do even when he took on various jobs. His parents, who divorced in 1926, were unable to help. By the end of 1927 he had left university.

It was a profound shock. Within the space of two years Wayne had been thwarted in his consecutive ambitions to become a naval officer and a pro football player. But he had already proved himself to be a well-rounded scholar—a

" WAYNE WAS KNOCKED OFF HIS BOARD BY A WAVE AND FORCED UNDERWATER.

resourceful, hardworking, and ambitious young man who excelled academically and on the sports field. These were attributes that would serve him well as he embarked on a whole new chapter in his life in the months and years ahead.

Images: Alamy, Getty Images

A BOOT IN THE DOOR

How the young Duke Morrison went from behind-the-scenes prop shifting to the cusp of stardom.

By NEIL CROSSLEY

For every actor that enters the profession through the time-honored route of drama school and stage, there are those with no training whatsoever who fall in by accident and go on to light up the big screen with their charisma and presence. They may not possess any finely honed drama skills at the outset, but they exude a realism, strength, and believability that resonates with audiences.

Such was the case with John Wayne, who after losing his football scholarship at the University of Southern California (USC) looked around for ways to make money. By then he had dropped the "Marion" from his birth name to become simply "Duke" Morrison. He had no thoughts of becoming an actor, but within months he was being drawn into an industry that fueled his interests and his talents.

It was Wayne's former USC football coach, Howard Jones, who helped secure him a job. Jones had given silent Western movie star Tom Mix tickets for USC football games. As a return favor to Jones, Hollywood director John Ford agreed to hire the young Duke as a prop boy and laborer at Fox Studios. Ford would become pivotal to Wayne's acting career. Decades later, Wayne would refer to Ford as "the most profound relationship of my life and, I believe, my greatest friendship."

As prop boy, Wayne joined a group of manual laborers known as a "swing gang" who were responsible for moving equipment and furniture and handling props.

Away from the elitist fraternity houses of USC, Wayne reveled in the rough and tumble of the blue-collar workforce. "There were a lot of tough guys around in those days, working in the picture business," he said years later.

At around the same time, silent actor Tom Mix allegedly introduced Wayne to Wyatt Earp, who was living out his days in Los Angeles. The legendary lawman and gambler made a real impact on a young Wayne.

"My father said he basically played Wyatt Earp," recalled Wayne's son Ethan on the American Heroes Channel in 2016. "When he has to play a sheriff or leader going into something, he goes in like he's Wyatt Earp."

In Scott Eyman's biography *John Wayne: The Life and Legend*, stuntman Yakima Canutt said that Wayne's behind-the-scenes exposure to genuine hard men played a major role in his presence on the screen. "He thrived on working with cowboys," said Canutt. "He picked up on what those men were like and he'd find ways of bringing those things into his pictures."

By 1928, Wayne began picking up work as an extra as well as bit parts at Fox and other studios. When a call went out for 6-foot-plus-tall extras for Warners' biblical epic *Noah's Ark*, Wayne put himself forward for the spectacular flood sequence. It was perilous work, with rivers of water and a mocked-up temple washing over Wayne and other extras.

Ford saw talent in Wayne and began molding him for parts. When Ford was assigned a film called *Salute*, his first "talkie," he enlisted Wayne's help to use some of his former USC football players in bit parts. Wayne played a naval cadet named Bill and the film features his first spoken line of dialogue.

As a prop man, Wayne earned $35 a week, but the salaries for *Salute* were between $50 and $75 a week. The only acting experience Wayne had was a few high school and college theater productions. In the years that followed, Ford would coach him in the pivotal skills needed by a screen actor.

"Duke . . . was just a stick of wood when he came away from USC," said director Allan Dwan in Eyman's biography. "Jack [John Ford] gave him character."

Wayne endeared himself to Ford by doing pretty much anything the director asked him to do, as demonstrated on the set of the submarine war drama *Men Without Women*, which was shot off Catalina Island in 1929. The scene required some of the actors to jump off a ship, disappear underwater, inhale some air from a submerged hose, then reappear gasping as though they were shipwrecked sailors.

In the normally sun-baked environs of Catalina Island (located off the coast of Southern California), it could almost have sounded like an enthralling aquatic game.

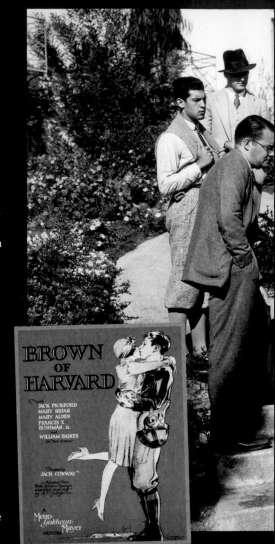

Director John Ford.

American actor Tom Mix.

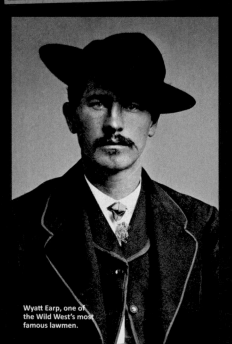

Wyatt Earp, one of the Wild West's most famous lawmen.

Below Left Wayne's first film, *Brown of Harvard*, was a silent movie.

Wayne makes his point in the 1931 film *Maker of Men*.

George O'Brien and Dolores Costello try to escape the flood in *Noah's Ark*, 1928.

WALSH WANTED AN UNKNOWN ACTOR AS THE STAR.

But on the day of the shoot the waves were high, the water was cold, and the skies were grey and forboding. The actors on the deck were far from enthusiastic, as Ford recalled years later.

"Our stuntmen, who were supposed to come up in bubbles, like they'd been shot out of an escape hatch, said it was too rough to work," recalled Ford. "Well, Duke was standing on the top deck of this boat we were on. He wasn't supposed to go in the water at all, but I asked him if he'd try this stunt. He never said a word except "sure." Dove right into the water from that deck. I knew right then the boy had the stuff and was going places. I could see that here was a boy who was working for something— not like most of the guys, hanging around to pick up a few bucks. Duke was really ambitious and willing to work."

Ford wasn't the only director impressed by Wayne. That same year, the director Raoul Walsh noticed Wayne lugging furniture around a set. Walsh was casting for his forthcoming Western *The Big Trail* (1930) and was convinced that Wayne had what it took for a starring role.

"He was in his early twenties—laughing, and the expression on his face was so warm and wholesome that I stopped and watched."

Walsh wanted an unknown actor as the star. When the studio balked at Walsh's idea, he replied, "I don't want an actor. I want someone to get out there and act natural—be himself. I'll make an actor out of him if need be."

The studios wanted a screen name for the young Duke Morrison though. Walsh suggested "Anthony Wayne," after

the Revolutionary War general "Mad" Anthony Wayne. Fox Studios head Winfield Sheehan rejected it, feeling it sounded "too Italian." Walsh then suggested "John Wayne," to the satisfaction of the studio. Wayne was accepted for the role and his pay was raised to $105 per week.

The Big Trail was the first big-budget outdoor spectacle of the sound era, costing two million dollars to make. Hundreds of extras were hired for the production, which was shot over the wide vistas of the American Southwest. Wayne starred as upstart fur trapper Breck Coleman, who leads a group of trappers through the treacherous Oregon Trail. His performance is stiff,

Wayne and Barbara Stanwyck in *Baby Face.*

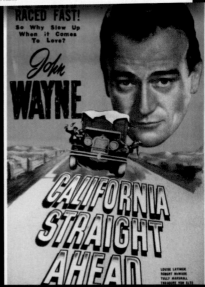

THE FILM WAS A FLOP AND THE BIGGEST CASUALTY WAS WAYNE.

but he was certainly hampered by the fact that Fox Studios were concerned about his diction, going so far as to hire a speech therapist, Lumsden Hare, to make Wayne sound like an Englishman. It didn't work.

To take advantage of the breathtaking scenery, the film was shot in two versions—a standard 35-mm version and a revolutionary 70-mm widescreen film process called Grandeur. Fox Studios were gambling on audiences being wowed by this new format, but few theaters were equipped to show the film in its widescreen version. As a result, the film was an enormous flop and the biggest casualty was Wayne. Had the film succeeded, he would undoubtedly have become a star. Instead, he was cast back into obscurity.

For the next eight years, Wayne was relegated to work in small roles in A-pictures, such as Columbia's *The Deceiver* (1931), in which he played a corpse. He appeared in the serial *The Three Musketeers* (1933). He also appeared in numerous so-called "Poverty Row" Westerns. One of the main innovations

that Wayne is acknowledged for was in allowing the good guys to fight as convincingly as the bad guys. Stuntman Yakima Cunutt and Wayne perfected onstage fight techniques that prevail to this day.

"Before I came along, it was standard practice that the hero must always fight clean," said Wayne. "The heavy was allowed to hit the hero in the head with a chair or throw a kerosene lamp at him or kick him in the stomach, but the hero could only knock the villain down politely and then wait until he rose. I changed all that. I threw chairs and lamps. I fought hard and I fought dirty. I fought to win."

By his own estimation, Wayne appeared in over 80 of these "horse operas" from 1931 to 1939. That could easily have been the culmination of his acting career—a steady yet wholly unexceptional body of work that paid reasonably well but would ultimately ensure his name was little more than a footnote in the annals of movie history. But director John Ford had not forgotten him, and in 1939 he would offer Wayne a project that would utterly transform his fortunes.

Dressed in buckskins and holding a rifle, Wayne performs in his first leading role in *The Big Trail*.

S T A G E
THE   DUKE'S

After eight years in B-movie wilderness, Wayne landed the role that would transform his fortunes.

★ ★ ★ ★

By NEIL CROSSLEY

Very few actors get two big breaks in the course of their careers, but that's what happened to John Wayne. Following the colossal flop of the *The Big Trail* in 1931, Wayne spent the following eight years relegated to B-movies and bit parts. Then, in 1939, fortune came knocking once again in the form of John Ford's landmark Western, *Stagecoach*.

Wayne had been completely demoralized when *The Big Trail* had failed at the box office, but had been bolstered by some sage advice from actor Will Rogers, who Wayne met one day on the Fox Studios lot. Wayne looked so miserable that Rogers asked him what was wrong. When Wayne told him, Rogers simply said, "You're working aren't you? Just keep working." Wayne later said this was "the best advice I ever got . . . just keep working and learning, however bad the picture . . . and boy, I made some lousy pictures."

Ford cast Wayne in the key role of the Ringo Kid, but there were objections from producer Walter Wanger and United Artists studio executives about Wayne's B-movie status. To pacify them, Ford allegedly said, "We can get him for peanuts." But Ford was shrewd. He had been watching Wayne's so-called "Poverty Row" films, and sensed how his talent might be properly developed if showcased properly.

Wayne himself had serious doubts about whether he could be convincing in the part, but he acknowledged that the role of the Ringo Kid was offered to him at "just about the time I was ready to resign myself to being a run-of-the-mill actor for the rest of my life." He also recognized the huge commitment that Ford made. "Everybody

COACH BIG BREAK

In this spectacular scene, Yakima Canutt leapt from a galloping horse to grab onto the horses leading the wagon before being "shot" and falling off.

told Ford he was committing suicide," recalled Wayne, "risking a third-rate bum like me in a million-dollar movie."

Ford chose to shoot the film in Monument Valley, Arizona, which became one of his favorite locations. From the outset he treated Wayne with noticeable cruelty. This was part of Ford's plan to break some of Wayne's bad acting habits and instill sympathy for him among other cast members, such as Claire Trevor, Thomas Mitchell, and John Carradine, so that they would help him to get his performance right.

Wayne poses with co-star Claire Trevor.

The ploy worked. *Stagecoach* in effect resurrected the careers of both Wayne and Ford. It's an outstanding achievement, a sweeping and powerful drama that charts the journey of eight disparate characters between two frontier towns. Along the way, they fend off attacks by the Apache.

The passengers are a fascinating mix: Claire Trevor plays Dallas, a prostitute forced to leave town; driver Andy Devine is a gambler; and John Carradine plays an inebriated frontier medic. Wayne, meanwhile, as the Ringo Kid, is a wanted murderer being escorted to prison.

Despite his past, there is a decency to the Ringo Kid. While the other passengers shun Dallas due to her profession, he insists on her being given the same water rations and a place at the table. He inevitably falls in love with her, which inspires one of the film's great scenes.

In *Stagecoach*, Wayne brought elements of character that would inform many of his subsequent roles: a tough honesty and integrity, unquestionable courage, and what the Sky History Channel referred to as "a laconic, almost plodding manner."

Wayne's first scene is iconic and unforgettable, as US film critic Emanuel

Levy notes in a review of the film on his website *emanuellevy.com*.

Levy cites how the Ringo Kid appears on the screen seemingly "out of nowhere" when he stops the stagecoach. The passengers ask, "Who are you?" to which he replies, "The Ringo Kid. That's what my friends call me. But my real name's Henry." Wayne's performance has real resonance. "Those three sentences," he recalled, "were my passport to fame."

In many ways, this is a morality tale played out across the large ensemble cast, a parable of sorts exploring complex psychological and moral issues via a simple narrative. For all the suspense and adventure, there's also a real tenderness to Ford's direction and comedic touches throughout.

The premiere of *Stagecoach* took place at the Fox Westwood Theatre in Los Angeles on February 2, 1939. Wayne recalled that when the film finished, an impressed

Director John Ford positions a camera atop a wagon.

 'HE'LL BE THE BIGGEST STAR EVER,' FORD HAD PREDICTED.

A scene from *Stagecoach*.

Wayne as the Ringo Kid.

audience "yelled and screamed and stood up and cheered. I never saw anything like that."

The film was released one month later, and it would prove to be a huge box-office success, grossing 1.1 million dollars. The film also received instant critical acclaim. Wayne as the film's anti-hero was singled out for praise.

He was likeable and convincing in the role and he more than vindicated Ford's faith in him. "He'll be the biggest star ever," Ford had predicted, "because he is the perfect 'everyman.'"

This was the first time that critics had acknowledged Wayne's presence and really praised his acting. A journalist for the *New York Daily News* echoed the sentiments of many when he wrote, "John Wayne is so good in the role of the outlaw that one wonders why he has had to wait all this time since *The Big Trail* for such another opportunity."

Stagecoach is a classic Western, one that revitalized the genre and injected realism and respectability into it. It was the film that made Wayne a major star

and pulled him out of the creative abyss of the B-movie Westerns. The film also demonstrated, for the first time, his abilities as a prominent screen figure who could "carry" a film.

Stagecoach was the film that really launched his career. It guaranteed that from that point on, Wayne was a critically lauded and commercially bankable, big-budget A-list actor. The former prop boy with dreams of fame had, almost overnight, become a household name.

CHAPTER 2

★

A NEW FRONTIER

AMERICA'S FAVORITE COWBOY

From Westerns to war films, John Wayne's star was firmly rising in the 1940s.

By NEIL CROSSLEY

he 1940 Academy Awards were particularly poignant for John Wayne. *Stagecoach* had made him an A-list star and in a year dominated by *Gone with the Wind* and *Mr. Smith Goes To Washington*, the film received seven Oscar nominations and won two.

Amid the tuxedos and ball gowns at the awards ceremony in the Ambassador Hotel, on February 29 of that year, Wayne was viewed as an actor of real promise.

The success of *Stagecoach* sparked a resurgence in Westerns, and studio heads clamored to sign Wayne up. He remained at Republic Pictures and by 1940 was focusing on films more befitting of his new A-list status. The first of these was *Dark Command*, in which he teamed up again with Raoul Walsh, who had directed him a decade earlier in the big-budget epic widescreen Western *The Big Trail*.

Dark Command is based on the book by W.R. Burnett about Quantrill's Raiders, a group of pro-Confederate partisan guerrillas who fought in the American Civil War. Wayne plays Bob Seton, a marshal of a Kansas town who is captured by the guerillas and faces execution.

Dark Command was a critical and commercial success, which encouraged Republic Pictures to allocate greater budgets for future John Wayne films. The film was the first of 16 Westerns that Wayne would star in during the 1940s.

The outbreak of the Second World War in 1939 sparked a wave of war dramas. Wayne appeared in nine such films in the 1940s, the first of which was *The Long Voyage Home* (1940), directed by John Ford. It's a powerful and moving episodic film about the tough, hard-drinking crew of a British steamer who transport munitions from the West Indies to England to help the British war effort. Wayne stars as Ole Olsen, a young Swedish farmer who winds up as a member of the steamer's crew.

Despite losing $224,336 at the box office, the film was widely praised by critics. Bosley Crowther, the film critic for *The New York Times*, concluded that, "It is one of the most honest pictures ever placed upon

Starring as Ole Olsen in 1940's
The Long Voyage Home.

Embracing actress Claire Trevor in *Dark Command*.

As Jim Gordon in *Flying Tigers*.

" HE WAS AN OBVIOUS CHOICE FOR ROLES DEPICTING STORIES OF VALOR DURING WAR.

Alongside Marlene Dietrich in *Seven Sinners*.

the screen . . . it shows that out of human weakness there proceeds some nobility."

Playing the sweet-natured Olsen was an atypical role for Wayne. However, it is one of his finest early performances and served to highlight his commanding screen presence.

In 1940, Wayne made the first of three movies with Marlene Dietrich. They appeared together in *Seven Sinners* (1940), with Wayne playing a naval officer and Dietrich the woman who sets out to seduce him. Although Wayne was married, he and Dietrich became romantically involved and remained good friends when their relationship ended. They would go on to make two more films: *The Spoilers* and *Pittsburgh* (both released in 1942).

In 1941, Wayne appeared in his first movie in color, *The Shepherd of the Hills*, directed by Henry Hathaway, who three decades later would direct Wayne in *True Grit*. Wayne stars as Matt Matthews, a hot-headed mountain man who develops an obsessive hatred for a supposedly messianic stranger.

It's a compelling drama, in which mountainous California locations provide a striking backdrop to the deft plotline. Hathaway's direction builds the tension beautifully and Wayne is impressive as the

Saddled up in 1943's
In Old Oklahoma,
(a.k.a. *War of the Wildcats*).

BELOW Wayne and Paulette Goddard
in *Picturegoer* magazine.

Picturegoer

John WAYNE & Paulette GODDARD

troubled Matt. As film critic Emanuel Levy put it, "Matt represented one of Wayne's richest characters to date."

When America entered the war in December 1941, Wayne was exempt from service due to his age and the fact he had a family. But he was an obvious choice for roles depicting stories of valor during the war.

In 1942, he starred in *Flying Tigers* as Captain Jim Gordon, the leader of a motley squadron of volunteer pilots who took on Japanese aircraft in the skies over China during the second Sino-Japanese War.

The film was well received due to the thrilling aerial fight scenes, which were created by Republic's special effects department. But critics were less inspired by the storyline and the cast. A review in *Variety* concluded that the script was "threadbare" and that Wayne and the cast were "barely adequate."

His performance was far more memorable in the epic 1942 romantic adventure *Reap the Wild Wind*, a drama directed by Cecil B. DeMille and co-starring Ray Milland and Paulette Goddard.

Wayne plays Jack Stuart, the captain of a ship wrecked off Key West, while Goddard plays a Floridian ship salvager who falls for him.

The film was wildly successful at the box office and earned three Academy Award nominations. It's an unusual role for Wayne, as he plays a character with a noticeably dark side.

Like many Hollywood stars in the 1940s, Wayne appeared as a guest on radio programs, such as *The Hedda Hopper Show*. He also starred in his own radio show *Three Sheets To The Wind*, an adventure series about an alcoholic detective.

As Wayne's star status grew, so too did his potential as an endorsee of products for advertising. One of the first advertisements was for a company called Adam Hats, and by 1948 Wayne was endorsing Royal Crown Cola in an ad that plugged his latest film *Wake of the Red Witch*.

By the second half of the 1940s, Wayne's star was firmly rising. In 1947, he produced his first movie, the *Angel and the Badman*, but it was the 1948 Western *Red River* that really elevated his career.

The film is a fictional account of the first cattle drive from Texas to Kansas along the Chisholm Trail. Directed and produced by Howard Hawks, it stars Wayne as the Texas rancher who initiated the trail and Montgomery Clift as his adopted adult

Opposite Montgomery Clift in *Red River.*

Working on the film *Three Godfathers* under the direction of John Ford.

On the set of *Fort Apache.*

 RED RIVER WAS A MASTERPIECE AND IS WIDELY REGARDED AS ONE OF THE FINEST WESTERNS.

son. The dramatic tension stems from the growing feud between the two characters.

Much has been written about the on-set dislike between Wayne and Clift. It's not difficult to see why they clashed. The two were polar opposites in terms of their looks, beliefs, politics, acting styles, and sexuality.

This was Clift's first major Hollywood role and Wayne was not convinced that he was manly or tough enough for the part. Wayne allegedly burst into laughter when Hawks staged a fight scene between them. "Wayne simply could not take the scene seriously," wrote Patricia Bosworth in her biography *Montgomery Clift*, "something that privately infuriated Monty and probably inspired the superhuman intensity he brought to this battle with the Duke."

Despite the conflict, *Red River* was a masterpiece and is widely regarded as one of the finest Westerns of all time. *Variety* called it "a spectacle of sweeping grandeur" with "a first-rate script," adding, "John Wayne has his best assignment to date and he makes the most of it."

The film cemented Wayne's tough, gruff, and wholly individual onscreen presence and made him a top box-office star.

Director John Ford was so impressed with Wayne's performance in *Red River* that he is reported to have said, "I didn't know the big son of a bitch could act!"

Ford subsequently cast him in three more Westerns: *Fort Apache* (1948), *Three Godfathers* (1948), and *She Wore a Yellow Ribbon* (1949). In the latter, a 42-year-old Wayne plays US Cavalry captain Nathan Brittles, who on the eve of his retirement rallies his troops to face an impending attack.

It's a stunningly accomplished Western and features some of Wayne's finest screen moments. Two particularly emotional scenes stand out: when Brittles talks to his late wife's grave, and when he accepts a gold retirement watch from his men.

Wayne's reputation would reach new heights with his final film of the decade, the war drama *Sands of Iwo Jima* (1949). Wayne plays US Marine Sgt. John Stryker, who is hated and feared by his men. Only when they enter the fury of combat do they finally understand the reason for his rigid brand of discipline and appreciate that it will be the difference between surviving the war and certain death. It's a powerful war drama and a commanding performance from Wayne, who received an Oscar nomination for his role.

By 1950, Wayne had become the number one film star in box-office popularity, according to figures compiled by the film industry magazine *Motion Picture Herald*.

On the 100th anniversary of Wayne's birth, in 2007, film historian Rick Jewell wrote a retrospective of Wayne in the *USC News* arguing that the 1940s was the era in which Wayne's image was really defined.

"Even though Wayne had yet to ascend to the upper reaches of stardom, the 1940s were a crucial time for him, because the mythic forces that would coalesce around his image as the quintessential American male began to take shape during this period," wrote Jewell. "The post-war American public embraced the man and they would not let go of him."

Images Getty Images, Alamy

A REAL-LIFE GUNFIGHT

Being prevented from serving his country in WWII cast a heavy shadow over a fierce patriot.

★ ★ ★ ★

By NEIL CROSSLEY

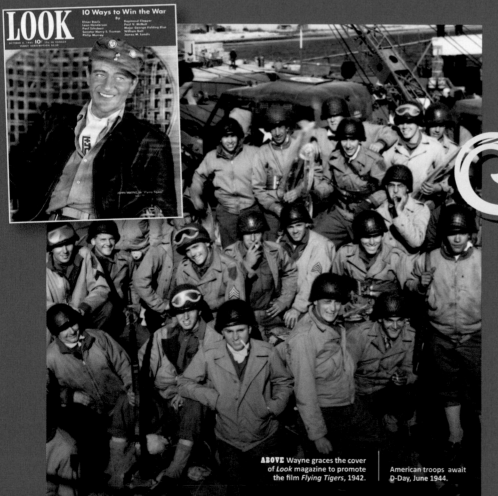

ABOVE Wayne graces the cover of *Look* magazine to promote the film *Flying Tigers*, 1942.

American troops await D-Day, June 1944.

America's entry into World War II prompted numerous Hollywood stars to enlist in the services. Jimmy Stewart was one of the first, becoming a colonel in the US Army Air Corps, leading a squadron of B-24 bombers and flying 20 combat missions over Germany. Clark Gable, Kirk Douglas, and Paul Newman also enlisted. John Wayne did not, and it would haunt him for the rest of his life.

It was December 7, 1941, when a Japanese aerial assault devastated the US naval base at Pearl Harbor, prompting the US to enter World War II. At the time, Wayne's second film with Marlene Dietrich, *Pittsburgh*, was days away from

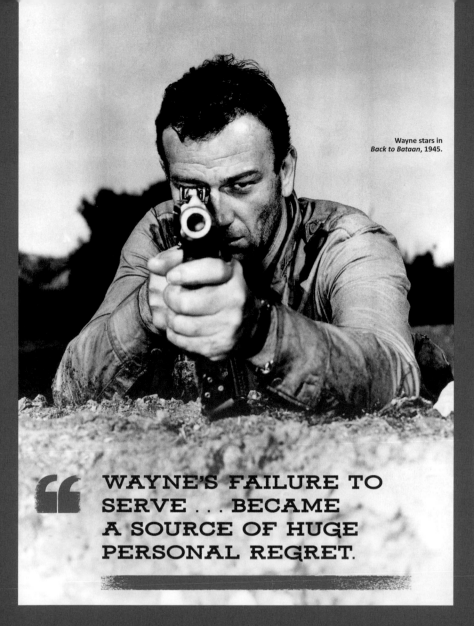
Wayne stars in *Back to Bataan*, 1945.

Wayne with his first wife, Josephine, on their wedding day.

Herbert J. Yates refused to lose his star man.

" **WAYNE'S FAILURE TO SERVE … BECAME A SOURCE OF HUGE PERSONAL REGRET.**

its release, and he was about to begin work on the romantic comedy *A Lady Takes a Chance* (released in 1943).

Wayne was exempt from service due to his age (34 at the time of Pearl Harbor) and family status (classified as 3-A—family deferment). He still attempted to enlist but Republic Pictures, terrified of losing their only remaining A-list actor, intervened, requesting Wayne's further deferment in the Selective Service conscription process. The president of Republic Pictures, Herbert J. Yates, even threatened Wayne with a lawsuit if he walked away from his contract.

At one point during the war, the need for more recruits prompted the US military to change Wayne's draft status to 1-A (draft eligible). But the studio intervened again, arguing that Wayne's star power was valuable for wartime

propaganda and a morale boost for the troops. He was then given a special 2-A status, which meant he was deferred in "support of national interest."

According to records in the US National Archives, Wayne did make an application to serve in the Office of Strategic Services (OSS), the precursor to the modern CIA. The OSS commander allegedly wrote Wayne a letter informing him of his acceptance into the Field Photographic Unit as a special forces commando. But this letter was sent to the home of Wayne's estranged wife, Josephine, and she never told him about it.

Wayne toured US bases and hospitals in the South Pacific for three months in 1943 and 1944. During this trip, he allegedly carried out a secret request from Colonel William Joseph Donovan to assess whether General Douglas

MacArthur, commander of the South West Pacific area, or his staff were hindering the work of the OSS. Wayne later received an OSS Certificate of Service from Donovan to commemorate his contribution.

Wayne's failure to serve in the US military during World War II became a source of huge personal regret for him, and accusations of being a draft dodger hung over him for the rest of his life.

In the post-war years, he gained a reputation as being fervently patriotic and right-wing, proactively supporting the Vietnam War against a tide of burgeoning liberal opposition. Wayne's widow, Pilar Pallete, suggested that his patriotism in later decades sprang from profound guilt.

"He would become a 'superpatriot' for the rest of his life," she wrote, "trying to atone for staying home."

TOP 10 FILMS

of the 40s

From Westerns to war, the forties saw Wayne transform into a big box-office star and earn a first shot at the Oscars.

★ ★ ★ ★ ★

By SCOTT REEVES

After the surprise attack on Pearl Harbor in December 1941, John Wayne was determined to contribute to the US war effort. He was exempt from military service due to his family status and age, but he would have been happy to volunteer. However, Republic Studios were adamant that they were not going to lose their biggest star. Wayne was threatened with legal action if he signed up, and the studio bosses pulled strings behind the scenes to ensure that

The
Fighting Kentuckian
1949

1940s

Wayne was not recategorized to make him eligible for the draft.

That left Wayne only able to serve his country on the big screen. *The Long Voyage Home* was his first war film, and it was followed by a host of others during the decade and beyond, including *Flying Tigers*, *The Fighting Seabees*, and the film that garnered Wayne his first Oscar nod, *Sands of Iwo Jima*.

Wayne's fiercely patriotic streak may have stemmed from a sense of guilt that he didn't serve during the war. He was offered the starring role in *All the King's Men* but refused since he believed the script was unpatriotic. It was a costly choice; the actor who landed the role, Broderick Crawford, beat Wayne to the Best Actor award at the 1950 Academy Awards.

 **THE LONG
VOYAGE HOME**
1940

 **FLYING
TIGERS**
1942

Though he may not look like a typical Scandinavian, Wayne adopted the Swedish persona of Ole Olsen for this wartime drama set on the high seas. The plot sees a steamship sail from the West Indies to England via Baltimore with a cargo of high-explosive shells, running the gauntlet of the Luftwaffe and Kriegsmarine. The crew uncover a potential spy in their midst, and Olsen looks forward to his eventual return to his homeland, a place he has not seen for 10 years. However, his crewmates must come to his rescue after Olsen is kidnapped at the end of the voyage and forced to serve on another ship.

The subject matter may have been a little too dark for many moviegoers, since the film made a loss on its cinematic release, although both contemporary and modern critics think it an excellent piece of work, and it was nominated for Best Picture at the Academy Awards.

 WOODY'S RECKLESS FLYING CONTRIBUTES TO THE DEATH OF TWO FELLOW AVIATORS.

Among the first of several films in which Wayne played an aviator, *Flying Tigers* tells the story of the American Volunteer Group (AVG) pilots who fought the Japanese in China—although it alters the timeline somewhat, depicting the pilots in action before the attack on Pearl Harbor when the AVG only began flying combat missions two weeks after.

Wayne plays Captain Jim Gordon, the fictional squadron leader of the Flying Tigers, and the film depicts his travails in trying to rein in a hot-headed new recruit, Woodrow "Woody" Jason. Woody's reckless flying contributes to the death of two of his fellow aviators, but he redeems himself on a dangerous mission in which he pushes Gordon out of a stricken bomber before taking the controls and crashing into a crucial enemy supply train. The exciting flying scenes helped the film become a box-office success, taking more than 1.5 million dollars.

3

TALL IN
THE SADDLE
1942

Tall in the Saddle marked the
final time that Wayne played a
role alongside George "Gabby"
Hayes, a prolific Western actor
who paired up with Wayne on
15 occasions. It was also the
only time that Wayne appeared
alongside Ella Raines, one of the
decade's top female stars.

The film sees Wayne as
Rocklin, a newly arrived
cowboy in an Arizona town
where the locals are less than
welcoming. Rocklin must
investigate the murder of
a rancher and protect the
inheritance of his daughter
from scheming locals, while
Raines provides the fiery love
interest, Arly Harolday.

Befitting the source
material—a serialized novel
published in installments—the
film has plenty of set-piece
confrontations and cliff-
hangers. It ends with the
uncovering of the murderer, the
unveiling of a plot to take over
the ranches in the area, and the
cowboy finally getting his girl.

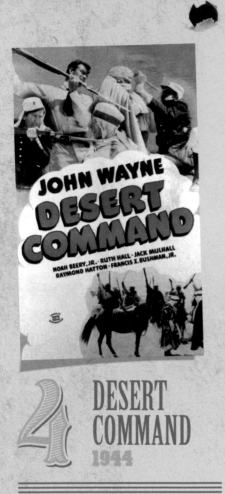

4 DESERT COMMAND
1944

Favorite Films jumped on Wayne's increasing fame by rereleasing a 1933 serial, *The Three Musketeers*, with a new title. The old version, a contemporary retelling of Alexander Dumas' famous story, was shown in 12 chapters, with a new one released to cinemas each week. It took some intensive editing to cut the 210-minute serial to a 72-minute feature. The result, *Desert Command*, is inevitably a little choppy. It also features some pretty limp acting from performers still learning their craft—not just a young, wooden Wayne, but future horror icon Lon Chaney, Jr., too.

Wayne plays Tom Wayne, an American pilot who rescues three French Legionnaires and searches for a mysterious Arab gunrunner and revolutionary. In celebrating the defeat of the wily Arabs and propping up the French colonial regime, *Desert Command* was a film that soon stood on the wrong side of history.

5 RED RIVER
1948

Red River saw Wayne as a tyrannical cowboy with Montgomery Clift—a future four-time Oscar nominee—playing his adopted son. Clift's character stands up to his father and ultimately wins his respect, but not before leading a mutiny on a long-distance cattle drive and starting a fistfight when they cross paths again. There were some (albeit far less violent) tensions on set too. Wayne doubted that the young Clift would be convincing as a rugged cowboy, but Clift's understated acting during their first on-camera confrontation settled Wayne's mind.

Two different cuts of the film exist. The first, a 133-minute pre-release, was edited down to 127 minutes due to Howard Hughes threatening legal action, since he claimed the ending was too similar his film *The Outlaw*. Director Howard Hawks later claimed he preferred the alternate version anyway, and *Red River*'s box-office success (it took 4.5 million dollars) suggests that audiences agreed with him.

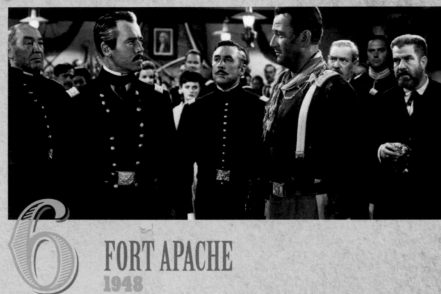

6 FORT APACHE
1948

Three of Hollywood's biggest stars came together in *Fort Apache*: Wayne as Captain Kirby York, Henry Fonda as Lieutenant Colonel Owen Thursday, and Shirley Temple as Philadelphia Thursday. Owen is an arrogant commander of Fort Apache who refuses to treat the local tribes with respect, driving them to rebel. York is the overlooked voice of reason.

Although the garrison is massacred by the Apache in scenes reminiscent of Custer's last stand at the Battle of Little Bighorn, the film was one of the first to present a more sympathetic portrayal of Native Americans: the battle is ultimately caused by the white Americans' disdain for them.

Fort Apache had a big budget (its three leading names were paid a fee of $100,000 each) but it still made a healthy profit, persuading director Ford to return to the Western genre again and again.

7 3 GODFATHERS
1948

Director John Ford adapted the novella *The Three Godfathers* by Peter B. Kyne for the big screen in 1919, releasing it as *Marked Men*. He returned to the same source material in 1948 for *Three Godfathers*. He cast Harry Carey, Jr., as the Abilene Kid; 29 years earlier, his father Harry Carey had played the same role. Wayne was Bob Hightower.

The story sees three bank robbers come across a woman, alone and in labor, as they flee a posse. They promise to look after her baby when she dies shortly after giving birth. Two of the robbers die too over the next few days, leaving only Bob to get the baby safely to the settlement of New Jerusalem.

It was a story familiar to audiences—not only was it loosely based on the three wise men of the nativity, but it also made it to the silver screen in two other adaptations released in 1916 and 1936.

" THE GARRISON IS MASSACRED BY THE APACHE.

JOHN FORD'S *Legend of the Southwest!*

JOHN FORD and MERIAN C. COOPER present

3 GODFATHERS

color by Technicolor

starring JOHN WAYNE
PEDRO ARMENDARIZ
and introducing HARRY CAREY, Jr.

WITH WARD · MAE · JANE · BEN
BOND · MARSH · DARWELL · JOHNSON

Directed by JOHN FORD

Produced by ARGOSY PICTURES CORPORATION
A METRO-GOLDWYN-MAYER PICTURE

8 SANDS OF IWO JIMA
1949

After more than 100 appearances on the big screen, *Sands of Iwo Jima* finally saw Wayne receive individual recognition from the Academy Awards. He was nominated for Best Actor, although he lost out to Broderick Crawford's portrayal of Willie Stark in *All the King's Men*.

Wayne's nomination came for his performance as John Stryker, a tough Marine sergeant who is haunted by personal demons and leads his men through a brutal training regime for which he is hated. However, Stryker's methods pay off and he earns his men's respect during the invasion of Tarawa in the Gilbert Islands, and later in the Battle of Iwo Jima. Stryker does not live to see the iconic raising of the Stars and Stripes after being shot during a lull in the fighting.

The film used veterans from the Pacific theater of the war as consultants and several real-life soldiers played themselves.

> [WAYNE] WANTED HARDY TO BE HIS REGULAR SIDEKICK.

9 THE FIGHTING KENTUCKIAN
1949

It's hard to imagine a bigger contrast between actors than that between John Wayne and Oliver Hardy of Laurel and Hardy fame, one a no-nonsense, all-American tough guy, the other a portly comedian with a quick wit and a ready laugh. Nevertheless, the two teamed up in 1949's *The Fighting Kentuckian*.

Wayne is John Breen, a militiaman who is sent out to survey unmapped land with Willie Paine, played by Hardy. The two bumble around Kentucky, foiling a scheme to deprive French army veterans of land granted to them by Congress.

The comedy-Western was something of a departure for Wayne, but he was so pleased with his and Hardy's onscreen chemistry he wanted Hardy to be his regular sidekick. However, Stan Laurel soon resumed his career after a break due to a diabetes diagnosis and Hardy rejoined him. The film was slated, which Wayne blamed on Vera Ralston being poorly cast as his love interest.

10 SHE WORE A YELLOW RIBBON
1949

The second in director John Ford's cavalry trilogy (sandwiched between 1948's *Fort Apache* and 1950's *Rio Grande*), *She Wore a Yellow Ribbon* was one of the most expensive Westerns ever made, with a budget of 1.6 million dollars. It made that back, and more—box-office takings were more than 2.5 million dollars.

The film depicts attempts to persuade native tribes to return to their reservations after their crushing victory at Battle of Little Bighorn in 1876.

Ford initially didn't want Wayne to play the main role of Captain Nathan Brittles, a grizzled veteran approaching retirement, since he thought Wayne was too young for the part.

However, Wayne's impressive performances in *Red River* and *Fort Apache* persuaded Ford to give him a chance. It would prove to be an inspired decision by the veteran director.

Although filming was tough, with cast and crew required to live in austere accommodation in Monument Valley (a desert on the Arizona-Utah border that is also home to an outlook called John Ford Point) both director and actor eventually considered *Yellow Ribbon* to be one of Wayne's best performances.

CHAPTER 3

★

MOVIE MAVERICK

Image Alamy

BEHIND THE CAMERA

A superstar by the end of the 1940s, Wayne
would dominate cinema in the following decade.

★ ★ ★ ★

By JOEL MCIVER

n many ways, the 1950s were the decade into which John Wayne fit best. Aged 43 in 1950, Wayne was in his prime as an actor, and because World War II had ended so recently, his pro-America, pro-conservative stance matched the public's appetite for security and stability. The mid 1960s—with the progressive trends that he later despised so much—was still an unimaginable distance away from the perspective of 1950, explaining why he was so prolific in this decade as an actor, producer, and box-office draw.

Wayne was able to pick and choose his projects at this point, having long been one of American cinema's leading men. He began the 1950s with a grudge match, declining the role of Jimmy Ringo in *The Gunfighter* (1950) simply because Harry Cohn, the head of Columbia Pictures, had treated him badly as an up-and-coming actor years before. "I couldn't stand the man," he later told the film critic Roger Ebert, although it's interesting to note that he paid tribute to Cohn's expertise in the same interview before revealing that he genuinely wanted the part of Ringo, which eventually went to Gregory Peck.

Shortly afterwards, Wayne declined the lead role in *High Noon* (1952), which—plot-wise at least—would have suited him perfectly, despite its somewhat progressive themes. He described it as "the most un-American thing I've ever seen in my whole life," with typical overstatement. Gary Cooper played the role that Wayne had rejected, winning a Best Actor Oscar alongside three others awarded to the movie.

To this day, it's the ultimate "John Wayne film that never was"—although he had plenty of other movies on his plate at the time and doubtless wasted little time worrying about it.

In fact, Wayne turned out some bona fide cinematic epics as the 1950s passed. His partnership with director John Ford led to *Rio Grande* in 1950, the last of Ford's "cavalry trilogy": Wayne played the hard-bitten Lieutenant-Colonel Kirby Yorke, who plays out a military and family drama against an attacking tribe of formidable Native Americans.

Western movies remained Wayne's stock-in-trade, of course, but he also played World War II heroes throughout the decade, as in the role of a submarine commander that he delivered in *Operation Pacific* (1951). He also took to the skies in airman roles in *Flying Leathernecks* (1951), *Island in the Sky* (1953), *The Wings of Eagles* (1957), and *Jet Pilot* (1957).

Surrounded by fans at the opening of Republic House in Soho Square, London, 1951.

Wayne with his sons Patrick and Michael on location in Mexico for the film *Hondo*, 1953.

A man on a mission in *The Searchers*.

With daughters Melinda (left) and Antonia Wayne.

> **[WAYNE] DELIVERED WHAT IS WIDELY REGARDED AS HIS BEST-EVER MOVIE PERFORMANCE IN ...** *THE SEARCHERS*.

For Wayne, the first half of the 1950s was essentially about reinforcing the tough, duty-driven, principled figure that he had embodied in his earlier career. While his films from this period have merit, they don't stand up to scholarly analysis beyond an appreciation of their basic themes. For example, in *The Quiet Man* (1952) Wayne plays a retired boxer; in *Big Jim McLain* (also 1952) he's a communist-hunting cop; and in *Trouble Along the Way* (1953) he's a college football coach. These are all solid, simple, conservative roles designed to supply family entertainment and a few dramatic thrills.

This changed in 1956, a year of highs and lows for Wayne, who delivered what is widely regarded as his best-ever movie performance in John Ford's *The Searchers*. Not only is it Wayne's high-water mark as an actor, it is regularly included among Greatest Western Films lists and even in Greatest Films of All Time collections. In the unlikely event that you haven't seen this masterpiece, here's a summary: it's the story of a soldier, Ethan Edwards, who returns in 1868 from eight years of warfare to his family settlement in the dramatic savannah of West Texas.

Smoldering, conflicted, and torn by opposing loyalties, Edwards embarks on a surprisingly brutal revenge spree when his niece is abducted: the character's arc is nuanced by Wayne's excellent performance. In the end, Edwards neither wins nor loses, a satisfyingly ambiguous outcome for the Western genre, hitherto a largely good-guys-versus-bad-guys world. Themes of racism, betrayal, and loyalty make *The Searchers* a deeper work than much of Wayne's earlier, and indeed later, films.

American comedian Red Skelton fights over a trophy with Wayne, 1953.

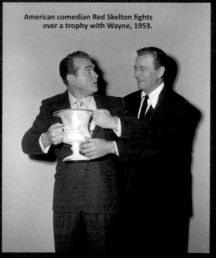

Wayne as Genghis Khan in *The Conqueror*, 1956.

MIGHTY IN SCOPE
...*mighty* as this man whose conquests changed the face of the world!

When the great motion pictures of 1956 are talked about...this one will be mentioned first!

HOWARD HUGHES presents
JOHN WAYNE · SUSAN HAYWARD
THE CONQUEROR
CINEMASCOPE TECHNICOLOR

2 YEARS IN THE MAKING...AT A COST OF $6,000,000

"THE WORLD? I WILL TAKE IT!"   "THE WOMAN? I WILL TAME HER!"

(L to R) Wayne, Maurice Chevalier, Anthony Quinn, and Jerry Wald during the 1958 Academy Awards rehearsals.

However, 1956 was also the year of *The Conqueror*, in which Wayne dons a laughable moustache to play the role of Genghis Khan and delivers the cheesiest of lines ("Your hatred will kindle into love . . . Your treacherous head is not safe on your shoulders!") with little attempt at a non-American accent. The film has been included on many lists of worst movies since its release, but *The Conqueror*'s legacy is rather less amusing than its content. Allegations, never really proven but never dispelled either, exist that many of its cast and crew developed cancer after working on the film, which was shot in St. George, Utah near nuclear test sites.

People magazine published research in 1980 that revealed that of the 220 film crew members, 91 developed various cancers, while 46 of those died from it. Dr. Robert C. Pendleton, director of radiological health at the University of Utah, was quoted as saying, "With these numbers, this case could qualify as an epidemic. The connection between fallout radiation and cancer in individual cases has been practically impossible to prove conclusively. But in a group this size you'd expect only 30-some cancers to develop. With 91, I think the tie-in to their exposure on the set of *The Conqueror* would hold up even in a court of law."

Although no connection between the cancers and the filming was definitely proven, or a class action suit brought against producer Howard Hughes, Hughes is said to have felt guilty about the health scares, especially as he and his crew knew about the radiation threat at the location and even shipped 60 tons of local soil to Hollywood to use in reshoots, potentially making the danger much worse. He is said to have bought up every print of *The Conqueror* for 12 million dollars, preventing it from release: it only emerged after his death in 1976.

Wayne wound up the fifties with 1958's *The Barbarian and the Geisha*, notable

Wayne with wife Pilar and Clare Boothe Luce at the Screen Producers Awards Dinner, 1958

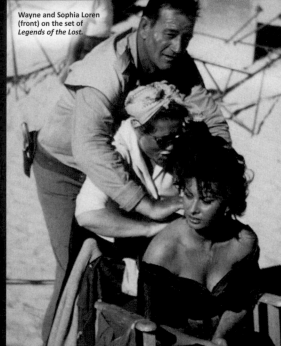

Wayne and Sophia Loren (front) on the set of *Legends of the Lost*.

" OF THE 220 FILM CREW MEMBERS, 91 DEVELOPED VARIOUS CANCERS WHILE 46 OF THOSE DIED OF IT.

primarily because he is said to have been in almost-constant conflict with director John Huston; the same year's *The Horse Soldiers*, in which he shared top billing with William Holden; and *Rio Bravo*, a superlative 1959 production by Howard Hawks that also featured Dean Martin, Ricky Nelson, and Angie Dickinson.

As well as acting, Wayne also established himself as a top-line producer in the fifties, founding a production company called Wayne/Fellows Productions in 1952 and subsequently renaming it Batjac. He got the name from Batjak, a company mentioned in the 1948 movie *Wake of the Red Witch* (a secretarial spelling error went uncorrected).

Although the best-known Batjac production is 1960's *The Alamo*, into which Wayne plunged much of his personal fortune, the company enjoyed successful business in the fifties, making *Big Jim McLain* (1952), *Plunder of the Sun* (1953), and 1954's *The High and the Mighty*, which won one of its five Oscar nominations. In 1955, Wayne paired with the great Lauren Bacall for *Blood Alley*, while Anita Ekberg starred in *Man in the Vault* (1956), and Sophia Loren stepped up for *Legend of the Lost* (1957).

After *The Alamo* and its slew of Oscars, Batjac was more sought-after than ever and, although times—and popular politics—changed, Wayne retained support in the industry and among the moviegoing public. Box-office successes included *McLintock!* (1963), *The War Wagon* (1967) with Kirk Douglas, the curious Vietnam war epic *The Green Berets* (1968), and *Chisum* (1970). Batjac continued into the 1970s with *Rio Lobo* (also 1970), *Big Jake* (1971), and three final films: *The Train Robbers* and *Cahill U.S. Marshal* (both 1973) and *McQ* (1974).

As we'll see, Wayne was really playing to type by the end of the sixties, but as long as the American public loved that type, all was well. It was only when that love affair ended that the road got rocky.

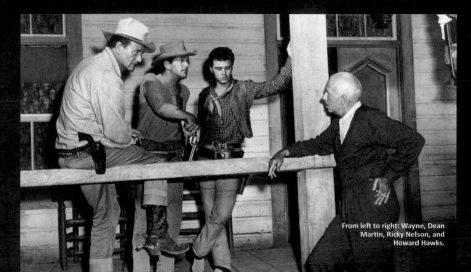

From left to right: Wayne, Dean Martin, Ricky Nelson, and Howard Hawks.

Images Getty Images, Alamy

LEADING
LADIES

Becoming a Hollywood heartthrob made it difficult for the Duke to stay faithful.

★ ★ ★ ★

By NIKOLE ROBINSON

At the height of his stardom, John Wayne held the hearts of women across America, but stories of his many marriages and infidelities were as well known as the ones he acted out on screen. It would seem that his celebrity status and desirability turned him into a womanizer, like with so many in Hollywood before and since, but he still managed to marry three times and be a loving father to seven children, creating the lasting but rather ironic image of a true American family man.

Wayne fell for his first wife while he was still pre-law student Marion Morrison attending the University of Southern California. He met Josephine Saenz, the 16-year-old daughter of the consul general of Panama, after a blind date with her sister, Carmen, and the two began a courtship. Her Spanish-American family disproved, as they were wealthy Catholics and Wayne was a poor Presbyterian. However, after landing the lead role in *The Big Trail* (1930)—opposite Marguerite Churchill, who he would again star opposite in *Girls Demand Excitement* (1931)—Wayne's fortunes improved, and he was finally given their blessing after seven years.

It's rumored that even before this big break, Wayne was already engaged in casual affairs with co-stars and coeds, but Saenz was perhaps unaware of this, hidden away in the ivory tower of high society. The couple were wed on June 24, 1933, in a garden ceremony and had four children by 1940, though their differing worlds of high society and Hollywood clashed, preventing wedded bliss. They disagreed on many things, including child-rearing and religion, and Saenz was also at odds with his long working hours and time away from the family.

Pictured here in his mid twenties, a dapper Wayne stands proudly beside his first wife, Josephine Saenz.

 IT'S RUMORED THAT EVEN BEFORE [HIS] BIG BREAK, WAYNE WAS ALREADY ENGAGED IN CASUAL AFFAIRS WITH CO-STARS.

By the birth of their fourth child they had truly drifted apart, with Wayne commenting that they were "moving in two different channels." However, he didn't feel divorce was the right thing to do for the family, instead spending even more time away from home to avoid conflict. Long hours "working" were likely in part to cover his philandering. But Wayne was always discreet, at least until he shot to fame in *Stagecoach* (1939). Now in the spotlight, rumors began to circulate. He was linked with four-time co-star Claire Trevor, Sigrid Gurie of *Three Faces West* (1940), British actress Merle Oberon, and Osa Massen, his accent coach in *The Long Voyage Home*

A strapping Wayne stars opposite Marguerite Churchill.

Wayne gets up close and personal with Claire Trevor in *Allegheny Uprising*.

(1940), among others, though mostly without proof. Undeniable, though, was his public three-year affair with superstar Marlene Dietrich. She began her pursuit of him after spotting him at Universal, pulling some strings to have Wayne cast opposite her in *Seven Sinners* (1940). Lovers both on screen and behind the scenes, Dietrich flaunted their affair, greeting him on set by jumping up and wrapping her legs around him, and they would brazenly attend events together without a care for public opinion or the studio-controlled press.

While on a trip to Mexico City in 1941, Wayne met Esperanza "Chata" Baur and began a two-year affair with the prostitute who would become his second wife. She was the polar opposite of Saenz—carefree

Sigrid Gurie.

Merle Oberon.

Osa Massen.

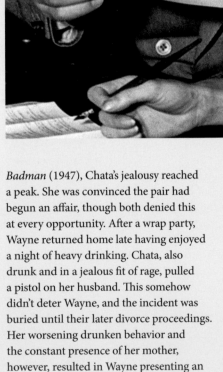

and passionate compared to pious and demure—and Wayne quickly fell in love with her, making frequent trips across the border. Upon Chata's moving to Hollywood in 1943, Wayne requested a divorce from Saenz, who had grown increasingly frustrated with her husband's disloyalty and distance. They separated in May 1943. Saenz was reluctant to grant him a divorce because of her Catholic beliefs, but by October she had realized the marriage wasn't worth saving. Wayne didn't fight her accusations in court, with Saenz granted full custody and generous support payments for both her and the children when the divorce was finalized on December 25, 1944. Their split affected their oldest son, Michael, most of all, who never forgave his father for deserting his mother and the family. "He's still angry at me," remarked the Duke in 1953. "I'm afraid he always will be. It breaks my heart."

Wayne and Chata tied the knot at Unity Presbyterian Church, Long Beach, on January 17, 1946, in a small, close-knit ceremony. With the studios having a great deal of control over the media, gossip and scandal was kept to a minimum to preserve Wayne's reputation as an American hero and family man, with the fact that the newlyweds had been living together for over a year kept tightly under wraps.

After a honeymoon in Hawaii, the lovers returned home, only to be greeted at the door by Wayne's new mother-in-law. Her presence would cause the first of many disagreements, with their home too small to comfortably house the three of them with any degree of privacy. He also began to have issues with the way Chata presented herself and her drinking habits, which would devolve into full-blown alcoholism. She, on the other hand, didn't like the devotion he had to his children and his career and grew jealous any time he was away.

When Wayne was cast alongside the beautiful Gail Russell in *Angel and the* *Badman* (1947), Chata's jealousy reached a peak. She was convinced the pair had begun an affair, though both denied this at every opportunity. After a wrap party, Wayne returned home late having enjoyed a night of heavy drinking. Chata, also drunk and in a jealous fit of rage, pulled a pistol on her husband. This somehow didn't deter Wayne, and the incident was buried until their later divorce proceedings. Her worsening drunken behavior and the constant presence of her mother, however, resulted in Wayne presenting an

CHATA, ALSO DRUNK AND IN A JEALOUS FIT OF RAGE, PULLED A PISTOL ON [WAYNE].

Wayne and Chata playing chess at home, 1947.

A loved-up Wayne and Chata apply for their marriage license.

Relaxing with Gail Russell on the set of *Angel and the Badman*.

ultimatum: "Choose between your mother and me." After a separation, she chose him, though she would claim to miss her mother terribly and disappear to Mexico City to be with her.

A trip to Ireland to film *The Quiet Man* (1952) with Chata and his four children in tow would restore some stability, and on their return Wayne revealed he had purchased a much larger home that was more to Chata's tastes, but he still didn't feel things were steady enough to start the family she desired.

Soon the same problems arose. Chata resumed her drunk and disorderly behavior and seemingly had an affair with hotel heir Nicky Hilton while Wayne was on location in Hawaii. Fed up, Wayne escaped to Peru under the guise of location scouting. With history repeating itself, it was here he met his future third wife, Peruvian actress Pilar Pallete, becoming quickly enamored by her sweet nature after years with the combative Chata. He would encounter her again the

next year in Hollywood and continue the affair, desperate to get out of his broken marriage to Chata so he could once again begin anew. Chata had often threatened separation, but this time Wayne called her bluff: "I've taken all I can take. I refuse to be a doormat any longer."

Unlike his semi-amicable split from Saenz, Chata weaponized the proceedings, claiming

Wayne carries his third wife, Pilar Pallete, along the runway after disembarking from a TWA flight.

Wayne takes a break from filming to walk with Pilar and their son, Ethan.

Wayne and O'Hara tend to an infant in *The Wings of Eagles*.

Alongside his final partner, Pat Stacy.

that Wayne was an abusive alcoholic. She wanted to take him for all he had and destroy his reputation in the process, while he just wanted freedom. However, Pallete complicated things, as if Wayne was proven to be unfaithful and living with a mistress, Chata could easily humiliate him in court.

Pallete's devotion was truly put to the test when she discovered she was pregnant. Rather than involving Wayne in the scandal that would emerge if he became known as the father, Pallete had a clandestine abortion. All the while, Chata continued to drag Wayne's name through the tabloids right up until their court date.

LEARNING FROM THE MISTAKES OF HIS FIRST MARRIAGE, WAYNE KEPT HIS RELATIONS WITH STACY QUIET.

Taking the stand, she continued with her attack on his character until he simply couldn't take it any more. Finally, he gave his version of events. Though he worried as a man no one would believe Chata had abused him for years, there were many witnesses to her alcoholism, and the case was settled. Wayne married Pallete in Hawaii the same day his divorce was finalized, on November 1, 1954.

As Pallete was also part of the acting world, she took a great interest in Wayne's career. She kept him company on set and location but struggled with loneliness. She soon gave up her own career to have what she desired most—a family. Revealing her pregnancy to Wayne in 1955, he was thrilled: "This is my second chance at being a father," he confessed. "This time, Pilar, I swear I'll do it right." His older children were less thrilled with the news, with his daughter Toni in particular worried that they were once again being replaced. There was also an age problem. With Pallete just six years older than Michael, the two Wayne families would have an overlap of new children and grandchildren. Though Toni did have her father walk her down the aisle shortly after his and Pallete's daughter was born in 1956, his third wife was not welcome at the ceremony despite his protests.

Things did improve with time, and Wayne really did seem committed to being a family man later in life—though affair rumors, especially about his long-time friend and co-star Maureen O'Hara, were always floating around.

After a strong decade, Palette became unhappy about having to uproot herself and the children each time her husband had a film to shoot, and her final pregnancy in 1966 saw her choosing to stay home instead. By this time, the family had relocated to Newport Beach, but Wayne never really felt like he belonged there with them. He also disagreed with his wife's conversion to Christian Science, while she disliked his expectations of a perfect housewife, and the fact that he was always working. In 1967 they began sleeping in separate beds, and after one failed session of marriage counseling, they separated in 1973.

Though Wayne never divorced Pallete, he spent the last years of his life with Pat Stacy, his secretary, who was also 35 years his junior. Though Pallete offered divorce, he preferred their separation. Learning from the mistakes of his first marriage, Wayne kept his relations with Stacy quiet, mostly for the sake of his younger children, but also for his image. Despite her age, Stacy was there for him throughout his illness and final years, her support for him never wavering.

Wayne was a man who had many relationships with women over the years—both professional and otherwise—but the man himself stated that he never figured them out. "I still don't understand women," he said. "I don't believe there's man alive who does."

TOP 10 FILMS

of the 1950s

Boxer, pilot, sheriff, coach: Hollywood's hottest star proved he was more than a cowboy and dazzled audiences with some iconic fifties performances.

By SCOTT REEVES

By the 1950s, John Wayne was undoubtedly a big-league actor—so well known that he had a cameo as himself in Hal Kanter's 1958 comedy *I Married a Woman* starring George Gobel and Diana Dors. Wayne was also enough of a star that he could afford to pick and choose his projects.

Although he was eager to play the lead role in *The Gunfighter*, he refused to work for Columbia Pictures due to a fall out with boss Harry Cohn. Gregory Peck eventually took the role in the 1950 release. Wayne also refused the lead in 1952's *High Noon* after reading the script. He saw it as an allegory against the blacklisting of suspected communists and called it "the most un-American thing I've ever seen in my whole life."

Wayne took more control over his casting calls by co-founding a production company with Robert Fellows; it later became Batjac Productions after Fellows moved on. Unsurprisingly, Wayne was selected to star in most of its productions, beginning with *Big Jim McLain* in 1952. However, Wayne also began to spend time behind the camera and was credited as a producer in a handful of films in which he doesn't appear.

RIO GRANDE
1950

Wayne returned to the character of Kirby Yorke, last seen in 1948's *Fort Apache*, to play the now-promoted Lieutenant Colonel—although he seems to have gained an extra "e" at the end of his last name. Yorke is still battling marauding Apaches, but this time on the Texas frontier. Yorke must deal with the personal issues created by his son turning up as a new but underage recruit, with Yorke's estranged wife following to insist the boy returns home. Yorke succeeds in repelling several Apache attacks, rescuing a wagonload of captured children, and rekindling romance with his wife. Not a bad day's work.

Wayne was the only actor to transfer across from *Fort Apache*, but he did team up again with regular co-star Harry Carey, Jr., and made his debut with Maureen O'Hara. Wayne's son Patrick also made his big-screen debut as an 11-year-old boy.

OPERATION PACIFIC
1951

The writers certainly had some fun with this one. Based on the submarine war in the Pacific Ocean during World War II,

Operation Pacific sees Wayne as the second-in-command of USS Thunderfish as it rescues orphans and nuns from the Philippines, boldly attacks various Japanese vessels, is tricked by a supposedly surrendering enemy, and rescues downed American airmen.

When the submarine returns to base, Wayne becomes entangled in a love triangle with his ex wife and her new beau, a pilot who just so happens to be the brother of Wayne's submarine commander and—in

even more of a coincidence—is one of the fortunate pilots rescued by Thunderfish towards the end of the film. Now what are the chances of that?

Operation Pacific's riotous writing helped it to more than double its 1.5-million-dollar budget at the box office, although critics derided the far-fetched plot and lack of onscreen chemistry between Wayne and future Oscar winner Patricia Neal, who was 19 years younger.

3 THE QUIET MAN
1952

Director John Ford, best known for Westerns, persuaded Wayne and Republic Pictures to try something different with *The Quiet Man*, although the studio insisted that they film *Rio Grande* before flying across the Atlantic for a month of shooting in rural Ireland.

Wayne plays Sean Thornton, an Irish-American boxer who returns to the farm where he was born and falls in love with Mary Kate Danaher, played by Maureen O'Hara. What follows is a romantic comedy that lacks the usual action of Ford/Wayne films, although the climax is a long fistfight between Thornton and Mary Kate's brother Will, the baddie of the piece.

Now a cult favorite that still prompts tourists to visit the movie's scenic filming locations in County Mayo and County Galway, *The Quiet Man* also repaid Ford's faith by earning him his fourth victory in the Best Director category at the Academy Awards (he'd previously won the award in 1936, 1941, and 1942).

> **WHAT FOLLOWS IS A ROMANTIC COMEDY THAT LACKS THE USUAL ACTION OF FORD/WAYNE FILMS.**

4

ISLAND IN THE SKY
1953

The highlight of Island in the Sky comes early on—an aircraft crash hailed for its realistic special effects. Wayne plays the wartime captain of the plane who must keep his crew alive in plunging temperatures after his Douglas C-47 Skytrain comes down in an isolated frozen lake in Canada. It's loosely based on a real-life search-and-rescue mission flown by screenwriter Ernest Gann, who was stationed in Maine and Canada and piloted supply planes across the Atlantic during World War II.

Director William Wellman, himself a fighter pilot in World War I with three confirmed kills, won the first-ever Academy Award for Best Picture for *Wings* in 1928. He managed to bring out a softer side of Wayne in *Island in the Sky*—rather than saving the day with gung-ho machismo, Wayne's character must keep his crew's spirits up while they await rescue.

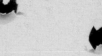

5 HONDO
1953

An early film produced by Wayne's new studio Wayne/Fellows Productions (later Batjac Productions), *Hondo* saw director John Farrow film with 3D cameras, although the equipment was temperamental and often broke down. As a result, Farrow avoided gimmicky 3D shots of objects moving towards or away from the camera and used 3D to increase the depth of wide landscape shots. *Hondo* was certainly a film with plenty of atmospheric locations.

Wayne plays Hondo Lane, a cavalryman whose unit is wiped out in an Apache attack and turns up at a homestead where a mother and young son are fending for themselves. The film explores the relationship between the US Army, white settlers, and the Apache. Geraldine Page was cast as Wayne's love interest and was shortlisted for Best Supporting Actress at the Oscars, the first time a 3D film was nominated in an acting category.

> **THE FILM EXPLORES THE RELATIONSHIP BETWEEN THE US ARMY, WHITE SETTLERS, AND THE APACHE.**

6 TROUBLE ALONG THE WAY
1953

Wayne took one of his rare forays into romantic comedy with *Trouble Along the Way*, in which sports coach Steve Williams—played by Wayne—tries to turn around the financial fortunes of an ailing Catholic college by setting up a lucrative football program. Williams must also try to hold on to his 11-year-old daughter, whose unscrupulous mother is fighting for custody.

Although the football team falls apart and a social worker writes a scathing report criticizing Williams, the Church agrees to keep funding the college and the social worker eventually works through her prejudices and gets together with Williams.

Donna Reed, best known for *It's a Wonderful Life*, took on the role of social worker Alice Singleton. The cast also features former professional basketball and baseball player Chuck Connors in one of the early roles of his 40-year Hollywood and TV career and an uncredited cameo by a young actor named James Dean.

Images Getty Images

7 THE HIGH AND THE MIGHTY
1954

Aside from Wayne as its star, *The High and the Mighty* shared many other cast and crew with the previous year's *Island in the Sky*: director William Wellman, screenwriter Ernest Gann, and several bit-part actors.

It also had a similar theme—in this case, Wayne is the first officer onboard a DC-4 airliner that experiences problems over the Pacific. The plane turns back in the hopes of reaching land, but Wayne is haunted by memories of a crash that killed his wife and son, and his captain is close to breaking point after years in the air. The passengers have their own problems and an argument leads to a pistol being drawn, but they eventually pull together and make it back to the safety of San Francisco.

There was a happy ending on the balance sheet too—the film made more than eight million dollars.

8 THE SEARCHERS
1956

Although largely ignored by voters during awards season, *The Searchers* has a good claim to be the best film Wayne ever made and was hailed by later critics—most notably, the American Film Institute named it the best Western of all time in 2008.

Once again, Wayne teamed up with John Ford and a host of familiar names, including Harry Carey, Jr. and Patrick Wayne, to film a big-screen adaptation of a Western novel.

Wayne plays Ethan Edwards, a Civil War veteran who embarks on a two-year chase through Texas to rescue family members who were captured in a Comanche raid. The tribal chief is eventually killed and Edwards' young daughter is returned home, although not before she has embraced Comanche culture. Wayne was so delighted with the film—one he described as his favorite role—that he named his youngest son Ethan.

"A STUNTMAN DIED WHILE FILMING THE CLIMACTIC BATTLE SCENE

9 THE HORSE SOLDIERS
1959

The Horse Soldiers was supposed to be a money-spinning blockbuster but ended up being a commercial failure. The plot, in which Wayne is a Union cavalry commander who leads a raid on a Confederate railroad depot, was fine. However, the project struggled to stay in budget from the start, not helped by both Wayne and co-star William Holden (star of 1957 hit *The Bridge on the River Kwai*) both receiving record $775,000 fees, plus a share of the profits.

US Open tennis champion Althea Gibson took a step into show business by playing a slave, but refused to speak in a stereotyped slave dialect. Then, a stuntman died after falling from a horse while filming the climactic battle scene and director John Ford lost interest, choosing to rewrite the end and conclude filming as soon as possible. The result was a film that lost money and was quickly forgotten.

10 RIO BRAVO
1959

Rio Bravo was Wayne's response to 1952's Western *High Noon*, which Wayne thought was un-American since it seemed to critique McCarthyism.

In contrast to *High Noon*, *Rio Bravo*'s hero, a Texas sheriff, is totally committed to his duty and refuses to accept the help of outsiders he deems disloyal.

Wayne plays Sheriff Chance, who arrests the brother of a powerful rancher and must keep him in custody until a US marshal arrives. The rancher lays siege to the jail and Chance must hold them off with the help of two former deputies (one a cripple, the other an alcoholic) and a young gunslinger.

Rio Bravo has a strong soundtrack, not surprising since it features crooner Dean Martin and young rock-and-roll heartthrob Ricky Nelson. Walter Brennan also contributes, winner of three Academy Awards for Best Supporting Actor (in 1936, 1938, and 1940 respectively).

CHAPTER 4

THE CONTROVERSIAL PATRIOT

POLITICAL

Wayne wasn't just satisfied with ruling the big
screen—he wanted to play a key role in deciding
who ruled America.

★★★★★

By JOEL McIVER

POWERHOUSE

Wayne and President Ford address
a crowd from the top of his limousine, 1976.

FIFTH REPORT

UN-AMERICAN ACTIVITIES
IN CALIFORNIA
1949

TO THE 1949 REGULAR CALIFORNIA LEGISLATURE
SACRAMENTO, 1949

Joseph McCarthy addresses a Senate Committee on communism in the US.

John Wayne was, as the saying goes, a bunch of different people: you can say the same about many actors. He was a family man, he was a business leader, and he was an outspoken commentator on many subjects. According to at least one biographer, he was a man to avoid when drunk, because that was when his outspokenness turned to ranting—and you really didn't want to be in his company when that moment came.

So what was Wayne ranting about? Well, there's a long list, and while a lot of the items on that list concerned the basic fact that modern America wasn't as courageous or as decent as it used to be, a lot of other things that bugged the man were of a political nature.

 A RUMOR PERSISTS TO THIS DAY THAT . . . JOSEPH STALIN WANTED [WAYNE] DEAD.

His early voting choices were relatively left-wing: he supported two Democratic presidents in Franklin D. Roosevelt and his successor, Harry S. Truman. Later, he explained that he had undergone something of a transition from left to right in his youth, saying in his *Playboy* interview, "In the late '20s, when I was a sophomore at USC, I was a socialist myself—but not when I left. The average college kid idealistically wishes everybody could have ice cream and cake for every meal, but as he gets older and gives more thought to his and his fellow man's responsibilities, he finds that it can't work out that way."

A lot of people experience a slight shift away from the left as they age and the unfair nature of life becomes obvious, but Wayne took this a giant step further. As the Cold War loomed in the fifties, a large sector of the American establishment became not just wary of the specter of communism but terrified of it, as

First Lady Mamie Eisenhower and Wayne at a political dinner, June 8, 1959.

He's a Go-Get-'Em Guy for the U.S.A. on a Treason-Trail that leads Half-a-World Away!

WARNER BROS. PRESENTS

JOHN WAYNE
THE BIG MAN IN HIS BIG ADVENTURE!
"BIG JIM McLAIN"
FILMED IN HAWAII AND FILLED WITH EXCITEMENT

NANCY OLSON · JAMES ARNESS

US President Richard Nixon (left) with Wayne (center) and Henry Kissinger in the White House.

Speaking at the Republican Convention in Miami, Florida, July 1968.

President John F. Kennedy.

Ready for action in *The Green Berets*, 1968.

evidenced by the formation of Senator Joseph McCarthy's House Un-American Activities Committee and its Hollywood equivalent, the Motion Picture Alliance for the Preservation of American Ideals.

Wayne supported the former and became president of the latter. His 1952 film *Big Jim McLain* featured himself in the starring role of a communist-hunting government agent.

In 1954, Senator McCarthy fell from grace as the US Government realized that he'd gone way too far with his anti-communist witch hunts. A rumor persists to this day

that the leader of the Soviet Union, Joseph Stalin, wanted Wayne dead for his anti-communist beliefs, although his films were apparently popular in the Kremlin.

Although the "Red under the bed" scare eventually receded from the American public imagination, Wayne was still appalled by what he regarded as a lack of morals in modern filmmaking. "The thing that will finally stop the movies from being an American habit is that parents have to guard their children against pornography . . . They make something dirty, and it makes

money, and they say, 'Jesus, let's make one a little dirtier, maybe it'll make more money.' And now even the bankers are getting their noses into it."

He also got behind the Vietnam War, itself an anti-communist exercise, by making *The Green Berets* in 1968.

When *The Green Berets* appeared in cinemas depicting a merry band of American troops as staunch, patriotic reliables of the type that Wayne had been

Images Getty Images, Alamy

Wayne signs Private First Class Fonsell Wofford's helmet during his visit to the 3rd Battalion, 7th Marines, at Chu Lai, Vietnam.

Governor Ronald Reagan (second from left) with Frank Sinatra, Vicki Carr, Nancy Reagan, Dean Martin, and Wayne at the governor's inaugural gala.

President Richard Nixon is greeted by Wayne during the US Presidential campaign, Miami, Florida, 1972.

 [WAYNE] FAVORED AND SUPPORTED . . . REDUCED TAXATION . . . [AND] THE FREE MARKET.

playing for decades, the liberal press gave it savage reviews, but the public lapped it up.

Instead, Wayne was asked to be the running mate for the Alabama Governor George Wallace, a candidate for the American Independent Party who supported pro-segregation policies. Wayne immediately rejected that opportunity, campaigning for Richard Nixon instead.

Wayne also got involved when ownership of the Panama Canal was a political issue. In the seventies, the then-Governor of California Ronald Reagan and others wanted the US to retain control of this crucial waterway.

Wayne, whose first wife had been Panamanian and who was close to that country's leader, Omar Torrijos Herrera, took the opposing view, writing to Reagan in 1977, "Now I have taken your letter, and I'll show you point by goddamn point in the treaty where you are misinforming people. If you continue these erroneous remarks, someone will publicize your letter to prove that you are not as thorough in your reviewing of this treaty as you say,

or are damned obtuse when it comes to reading the English language."

He based his assessment of American life, as he witnessed it in the middle of the 20th century, on the idea that pretty much everything was better in the old days. People were better; America was better; life was better. To that end, he favored and supported Republican policies such as reduced taxation, deregulation, the free market, governmental withdrawal from the everyday lives of the populace, and the general principle that quality will rise to the top.

THE ALAMO

It was the passion project of John Wayne's life.

★ ★ ★ ★

By NEIL CROSSLEY

I f anyone was going to make a film about the 1836 Battle of the Alamo, then it was probably always going to be John Wayne. The hard-fought victory by besieged Texans over the Mexican army has become enshrined in America's consciousness as a symbol of freedom against oppression, and this symbolism chimed seamlessly with Wayne's patriotic zeal.

Directing the action on
the set of *The Alamo*.

Wayne had been planning the film since 1945, when he hired scriptwriter James Edward Grant, but he clashed with Republic Pictures head Herbert Yates over the proposed three-million-dollar budget. Wayne left Republic, signed with United Artists, and formed the production company Batjac with producer Robert Fellows. United Artists contributed 2.5 million dollars towards the project and acted as distributor.

Other investors included Wayne himself, who put in 1.5 million dollars.

Wayne directed, produced, and starred in the film as Davy Crockett. He had intended only to direct and produce, but investors insisted he play a leading part. Wayne cast Richard Widmark as pioneer Jim Bowie and British actor Laurence Harvey as William Barrett Travis. Singer Frankie Avalon was also added in a bid to draw in a teen audience.

A recreation of the Alamo was built in a location near Bracketville,

Texas, but shooting was problematic: Richard Widmark complained he was miscast and threatened to leave; John Ford turned up unexpectedly, which challenged Wayne's authority; a cannon fell on Harvey's foot; crickets plagued the set; and Avalon was intimidated by rattlesnakes. But the biggest problem was the script. Many felt the film was a political platform for Wayne, with much of his onscreen dialogue as Crockett reflecting his anti-communist views.

Another major flaw was the film's historical inaccuracy. "There is not a single scene in *The Alamo* which corresponds to a historically verifiable incident," said Alamo historian Timothy Todish. It was a view shared by historians James Frank Dobie and Lon Tinkle, who demanded that their names be removed as historical advisers.

The film was released on October 24, 1960, to mixed critical reviews. *The New York Herald Tribune* concluded that it

THE
ALAMO
in TECHNICOLOR

JOHN WAYNE   RICHARD WIDMARK   LAURENCE HARVEY
RICHARD BOONE

" MANY FELT THE FILM
WAS A POLITICAL
PLATFORM FOR WAYNE.

Taking a break from filming with his daughter.

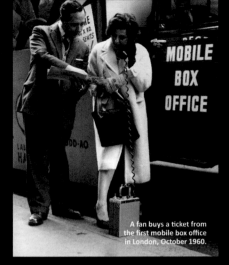

A fan buys a ticket from the first mobile box office in London, October 1960.

Wayne attends the première of *The Alamo*, October 1960.

was "a magnificent job." By contrast, *Time* magazine reported that it was as "flat as Texas."

While it fared well at the box office, its significant costs prevented its success. The film was nominated for seven Academy Awards, including Best Picture and Best Actor in a Supporting Role, and it won one for Best Sound.

Wayne invested over ten years of his life in *The Alamo* and took out second mortgages on his homes to fund it. This was the passion project of his life.

Decades later, Wayne's daughter Aissa, who appeared in the film alongside other friends and family members, reflected on her father's film. "I think making *The Alamo* became my father's own form of combat. More than an obsession, it was the most intensely personal project in his career."

FALSE ADVERTISING

How Wayne promoted the deadly habit that would
ultimately take his life.

★★★★

By NEIL CROSSLEY

s Wayne's reputation as an actor grew, so too did his potential as an endorsee for brands. By 1950, he had become the poster boy for Camel cigarettes. In one of the first such magazine ads, Wayne is seen in a checkered shirt, smiling and looking relaxed, with a cigarette in his right hand. "The roles I play in movies," begins the headline quote, "are far from easy on my voice—I can't risk throat irritation. So I smoke Camels—they're mild."

Wayne was a heavy smoker and by the mid 1950s, he was getting through six to seven packs a day. He also appeared in TV ads for Camel, such as one in 1952, filmed in conjunction with his forthcoming film *Big Jim McLain*. Such cross-promotion deals between the tobacco industry and Hollywood were common practice by then.

Up until the 1950s, neither doctors nor the public recognized smoking as a serious health threat. But in 1953, medical research into the link between smoking and lung cancer prompted a health scare in the US, with *Life* magazine and *Time* running major stories about it. By 1957, smoking had been conclusively proven to cause lung cancer, yet it took a damning report by the Surgeon General's Advisory Committee in 1964 for a significant shift in public attitudes towards smoking to take place. From that point on, the prevalence of smoking began a slow, steady decline.

It was also in 1964 that Wayne was diagnosed with lung cancer. By then Wayne was 57, and it was he who coined the term "the Big C" for cancer when announcing that he had undergone successful surgery to remove a cancerous left lung.

 IT WAS ALSO IN 1964 THAT WAYNE WAS DIAGNOSED WITH LUNG CANCER.

He seemed to be cured, but was severely short of breath and unable to exercise. Despite this he soon resumed chewing tobacco and smoking cigars. Fifteen years later he would be dead from stomach cancer at the age of 72. On April 8, 1979, two months before his death, Wayne made his last public appearance, at the 51st Academy Awards, where he received a standing ovation. "Thank you, ladies and gentlemen," he beamed. "That's just about the only medicine a fella would really ever need."

TOP 10 FILMS of the

1960s

The sixties saw Wayne recognized as the best in his profession, but not before a health scare that nearly ended his life.

★ ★ ★ ★ ★

By SCOTT REEVES

The 1960s saw John Wayne finally handed a golden statuette by the Motion Picture Academy when they recognized him as Best Actor for his role as Rooster Cogburn in 1969's *True Grit*. However, Wayne had a rocky decade before the high point of his acting career. Producing *The Alamo* was exhausting and financially crippling. Wayne's advancing age saw him becoming less suitable for many roles—romantic entanglements became rare, and he was 58 when he acted in his final World War II movie in 1965.

Yet the biggest problems that Wayne had to navigate were health related. Being a chain-smoker since he was a young man finally caught up with him in the middle of the 1960s. Wayne was increasingly hit by coughing attacks and found it difficult to breathe, especially while filming *In Harm's Way*. Shortly after the film wrapped, Wayne went under the knife for major surgery and there was a real risk he would never wake up. Thankfully he did, and he went on to quickly recuperate and resume his career in front of the camera. Director Howard Hawks even thought Wayne was a better actor after surgery because only having one lung changed the manner of his speech.

NORTH TO ALASKA
1960

This comedy, set during the Alaskan gold rush at the turn of the 20th century, tickled audiences and made a healthy profit, although it had a bumpy journey to the big screen. Wayne committed to the project as the first of a three-film deal with 20th Century Fox without reading a script, and the studio struggled to find a director. Filming was delayed by a writers' strike, and the screenplay was still not complete by the time the cast were on location in California, but it ultimately came together with the help of an emergency scriptwriter and a good deal of improvisation.

North to Alaska is perhaps best known for its theme song, which peaked at number four in the national charts. Sadly, singer Johnny Horton didn't live to enjoy its success; the 35 year old died in a car crash just eight days before the film's release.

 THE SCREENPLAY WAS STILL NOT COMPLETE BY THE TIME THE CAST WERE ON LOCATION.

2 THE COMANCHEROS
1961

Wayne drew upon his years of industry experience when director Michael Curtiz struggled during the filming of *The Comancheros* due to cancer.

On days when Curtiz was too ill to work, Wayne (who had recently directed *The Alamo*) took over directing duties and kept the project moving. Despite this, he refused a co-directing credit. However, he did stamp his authority on the set by making an assistant director remove a JFK supporter badge.

Wayne plays a Texas Ranger who must join forces with his captive (portrayed by Stuart Whitman) to defeat a criminal gang known as the Comancheros. After the captive helps to save the day, he is sworn in as a Ranger and helps to bring about the Comancheros' downfall. The gang featured Patrick Wayne in the cast (he was now a regular supporting actor in his father's films) and also included Wayne's five-year-old daughter Aissa.

HATARI!
1962

In *Hatari!* Wayne swapped the American West for East Africa. He plays Sean Mercer, one of an eclectic company of trappers (featuring a Mexican bullfighter, German racing driver, Native American sharpshooter, and a former New York cab driver) who catch wild animals for zoos and circuses.

The ethics of chasing animals in jeeps and trucks before transporting them to foreign zoos was far less controversial in the sixties than today, so director Howard Hawks used the dubious trade as the setting for a romantic comedy in which Wayne's game catcher falls for an Italian photographer.

The animals in the film were all wild and the actors performed the dangerous chases themselves with only a little guidance from expert animal handlers. When one rhino actually escaped, Hawks kept the cameras rolling and used the footage in the final cut, albeit with redubbed audio due to Wayne's loud cursing.

THE MAN WHO SHOT LIBERTY VALANCE
1962

The Man Who Shot Liberty Valance saw Wayne team up with director John Ford—nothing unusual there, the two men had made a career out of filming Westerns together—but also brought in James Stewart as a co-star, the first time Wayne and Stewart had worked together.

Ford was required to cut costs by Paramount Pictures. He switched back to black and white after shooting in color for the last few years, and filmed almost entirely on soundstages rather than on location. Perhaps the changes weren't to his taste, because the often-irritable Ford was even more cantankerous than usual, baiting his two A-list actors and leaving fellow cast member Woody Strode to describe it as "a miserable film to make."

However, the story of an up-and-coming lawyer-politician vanquishing a local hoodlum ultimately did well, more than doubling its 3.2-million-dollar budget, and in 2007 it was selected for preservation by the US Film Registry.

5 THE LONGEST DAY
1962

Although Wayne was the number-one draw in most of his films, he wasn't above taking a role in an ensemble, as he did in D-Day epic *The Longest Day*. That said, he negotiated hard before accepting a role initially slated for Charlton Heston, and which only took four days to shoot. Wayne got the highest fee of the entire cast ($250,000—around 10 times what the rest were paid) and insisted on a distinct billing ("and John Wayne") in the credits. Wayne plays Lieutenant Colonel Benjamin Vandervoort, who commanded paratroopers during the battle for Sainte-Mère-Église despite breaking his ankle on landing. The gallant veteran was reportedly unhappy that 54-year-old Wayne was cast to play him since Vandervoort was half his age on D-Day.

The Longest Day was a hit, drawing in enough punters to comfortably make a profit despite its mammoth cast. It was also nominated for five Oscars (winning for Best Cinematography, black and white) and won a Golden Globe.

> **"** [WAYNE] NEGOTIATED HARD BEFORE ACCEPTING A ROLE INITIALLY SLATED FOR CHARLTON HESTON.

6 HOW THE WEST WAS WON
1962

Soon after *The Longest Day* hit cinemas, Wayne featured in another ensemble epic, and it was also nominated for Best Picture at the Oscars—although release dates meant that *How the West Was Won* was shortlisted for the following year's ceremony so the two didn't go up against each other.

The 164-minute blockbuster followed one family's fortunes from 1839 to 1889, although Wayne only had to give up five days to film the role of General William Tecumseh Sherman (a character he also portrayed in 1960's *Wagon Train: The Colter Craven Story*).

Casting so many big names with busy schedules was a logistical nightmare. Wayne was initially put down to play an alternative part, but John Ford snaffled his favorite star for the Civil War section he was lead director for. Wayne was then touted to play opposite Spencer Tracy as Union general (and the 18th US President) Ulysses S. Grant, but Harry Morgan eventually landed that role and Tracy became the film's narrator instead.

7 McLINTOCK!
1963

The advertising poster for *McLintock!*—in which Wayne gives a public spanking to Maureen O'Hara in the name of comedy—is a clue that this film hasn't aged particularly well.

Wayne was heavily involved in the development of the script and pushed for a humorous allegory on Hollywood's stereotyped view of Native Americans, domestic abuse, and political corruption. The result is a slapstick comedy in which Wayne's character, G.W. McLintock, attempts to keep the peace between a corrupt government, local Comanches, ranchers, and his own feuding family.

O'Hara later claimed that Wayne was so enthusiastic in the infamous spanking scene that she had bruises on her backside for weeks afterwards—not that it stopped their onscreen characters from reconciling a few scenes later.

McLintock! raked in a whopping 14.5 million dollars in North America, helping to bring financial stability to Batjac Productions after the financial travails inflicted by making *The Alamo*.

Images Getty Images

IN HARM'S WAY
1965

8

A film that marked the end of an era, *In Harm's Way* was Wayne's last black-and-white film and his last set during WWII.

Wayne stars as Rock Torrey, a naval officer who is initially removed from command for recklessly chasing a Japanese submarine during the attack on Pearl Harbor, but is later recalled because his dauntless approach is necessary to capture a strategic island.

Alongside him is Kirk Douglas as Paul Eddington, a similarly wayward officer who

goes out in a blaze of glory, and Patricia Neal as Maggie Haines, a nurse and Torrey's love interest.

In Harm's Way isn't regarded as one of Wayne's finest performances, perhaps because the star was seriously ill and coughing up blood—though it didn't stop him fromsmoking six packs of cigarettes a day. He was diagnosed with lung cancer as filming wrapped; two months later he underwent

9 EL DORADO
1966

Film buffs had a déjà vu moment when first viewing *El Dorado*: director Howard Hawks and Wayne team up in a film in which a gang of good guys must defend a sheriff's office from corrupt ranchers. But *El Dorado* is more than just a rehash of 1959's *Rio Bravo*. It's a character piece that explores the motivations of Wayne's character, gun-for-hire Cole Thornton, and scriptwriter Leigh Brackett thought *El Dorado* was his finest piece of work. Robert Mitchum is an admirable co-star, while James Caan and Charlene Holt are among the supporting cast.

Although insiders were concerned at Wayne's ability to portray a physically active character like a Wild West gunslinger following lung cancer and major surgery, there were few signs that he struggled, although he increasingly relied on stunt doubles in any scenes that required exertion, even if his character only needed to run.

El Dorado was a commercial success, making almost six million dollars at the box office.

10 TRUE GRIT
1969

Wayne had the perfect answer to any doubters who thought his career would go into decline after his health scare: *True Grit*. The Western captured him the Academy Award for Best Actor after more than four decades on screen.

Wayne also showed that he was still capable of acting in physical roles—the stunt in which Wayne's character Rooster Cogburn jumps a four-rail fence on his horse to prove his prowess was performed by Wayne himself, although director Henry

> **[ELVIS PRESLEY] INSISTED ON TOP BILLING ABOVE WAYNE.**

Hathaway did choose to leave filming it until last in case anything went wrong.

Producers struggled to fill the other two main roles. The female lead was turned down by Mia Farrow and Karen Carpenter, among others, before Kim Darby took it. Elvis Presley was then slated to play Texas Ranger La Boeuf but insisted on top billing above Wayne, a demand that was refused. Fellow singer-guitarist Glen Campbell got the role instead and was Oscar nominated for the title song.

CHAPTER 5

★

A TROUBLING ICON

HOLLYWOOD
HERO

As the tides of progress rippled across the world, one leading
man remained resolutely traditional.

ike the structure of its title, *The
Alamo* was such a monumental
movie that it elevated its star John
Wayne to a whole new level on its
release in 1960.

As we've seen, he'd
enjoyed a pretty successful fifties by anyone's
standards, but as America embarked on its most
transformative decade yet, cinema's most rooted-
in-tradition star was about to make his mark
more deeply than ever before. There's an irony
there that Wayne's dry humor would no doubt
appreciate.

Wayne had never been so prolific: the roles
kept rolling on in, and he stepped into them
with alacrity. Also in 1960, he starred in *North
to Alaska* alongside Stewart Granger and Ernie
Kovacs: it's a Gold Rush comedy in which
the great man falls unexpectedly in love. The
following year, he shared top billing with Stuart
Whitman in *The Comancheros*, a movie whose
subject is immediately apparent from its title: still,
the tale of a Texas ranger forced to moonlight
from his command is worth your time.

In 1962, Wayne appeared in no fewer than
three films, and no matter how accomplished
an actor you may be, that is a feat of energy and
commitment that few thespians could match, let

alone at the age of 55. The first was John Ford's *The
Man Who Shot Liberty Valance*, a classic thriller in
which James Stewart also featured: there's a superb
twist in the tale, and an expert framing device, that
make it essential viewing for any Wayne fan.

A Howard Hawks production, *Hatari!*, followed,
which was shot in Africa. Wayne, playing the role
of an animal collector, was obliged to work with
real, living, biting wildlife—a pursuit that would be
illegal for many reasons today.

Finally for 1962, Wayne topped an ensemble cast
in *The Longest Day*, all of whom were paid a paltry
sum while he nabbed a fee of $250,000. Why?
Because the producer Darryl F. Zanuck had once
said something patronizing about him and was
therefore obliged to pay up or lose his mercurial
star. Who says that holding grudges doesn't pay off
in the end?

In 1963, the year that President Kennedy's
assassination shocked a nation already unnerved
by the near miss of the Bay of Pigs debacle the
year before, Wayne's stocky, unflappable presence
soothed moviegoers in three more productions.
The first was a segment of the epic *How the
West was Won*, a movie that took audiences back
to a time when America was new, brave, and
triumphant: he starred in the portion of the movie
directed by his mentor John Ford. Later that year

Shooting *Circus World* with Claudia
Cardinale, Madrid, Spain, 1964.

Wayne with his daughter
Melinda on her wedding
day, April 1964.

he led off his last Ford film, *Donovan's Reef*, in which Lee Marvin was his co-star. The year ended with *McLintock!*, one of many exclamation-marked heroic roles that populated the cinema of the day.

As the mid sixties rolled around, Wayne's roles diversified a little, simply because American cinema and the power structure in Hollywood was evolving. After all, the Beatles were making headlines nowadays, and long hair, a snarky attitude, and a fondness for raucous entertainment were becoming standard among moviegoers. However, this didn't stop him from tearing up movie screens with 1964's *Circus World*, alongside Rita Hayworth, as well as George Stevens' *The Greatest Story Ever Told* a year later, in which our man played a predictably no-nonsense Roman centurion.

After finishing 1965 in Otto Preminger's *In Harm's Way* and co-starring with Dean Martin in *The Sons of Katie Elder*, Wayne took a break, at least by his standards.

He delivered a brief cameo in Melville Shavelson's *Cast a Giant Shadow* in 1966, but rested up in time for another cinematic onslaught in 1967 with Kirk Douglas again, this time in Burt Kennedy's *The War Wagon*. Wartime themes prevailed in *El Dorado*, a remake of *Rio Bravo* with Robert Mitchum.

We've already talked about *The Green Berets*, Wayne's ill-fated 1968 attempt to set a movie in the midst of the ongoing Vietnam War. It probably seemed like a good idea on paper to insert a band of generic soldier boys and their tough-guy-with-a-heart-of-gold colonel into

 HE WAS TOO BIG TO FAIL AT THIS STAGE. ALTHOUGH THAT INVULNERABILITY WOULDN'T LAST.

Like father, like son: Ethan mimics his father during filming for *El Dorado*.

Attracting attention during a trip to Rome, 1965.

JOHN WAYNE
GLEN CAMPBELL
KIM DARBY
HAL WALLIS'

TRUE GRIT
A BRAND NEW BRAND OF AMERICAN FRONTIER STORY

In conversation with US troops at a checkpoint in Saigon, Vietnam.

the East Asian jungle, but it rubbed the wrong way against the growing liberal, anti-war sector of the political and intellectual populace, and the movie was doomed to fail.

Fortunately, Wayne walked away with his career intact: he was too big to fail at this stage, although that invulnerability wouldn't last. A solid 1968 movie called *Hellfighters*, in which he played a firefighter on an oil rig, undid some of the damage caused by *The Green Beret*s, and 1969's *True Grit* was an all-time Wayne classic, up there with *The Searchers* and *The Alamo* for fans of the Duke. In this much-loved Western, the rapidly aging star plays an old rascal called Rooster Cogburn in an expert performance that bagged him the Best Actor Oscar and a Golden Globe. It seemed that Hollywood and America's cultural establishment hadn't written Wayne off quite yet.

In fact, Wayne fairly sailed into the early seventies before ill health finally caught up with him, as it was bound to do given his bout with cancer in the previous decade and a larynx-shredding 60-a-day cigarette habit. 1970's *Chisum* was a decent film, with Wayne playing the part of a cattle ranch owner who applies extreme justice to a host of bandits. Perhaps a little bizarrely, a second remake of *Rio Bravo* arrived the same year titled *Rio Lobo*: this time out, Wayne portrayed an army colonel

who chases down a posse of no-good Confederate soldiers in the Civil War.

In 1971, Wayne earned more critical plaudits in George Sherman's *Big Jake*, in which he played a man tracking down a gang who had abducted his grandson. The film was a bit of a tearjerker, in fact, with Wayne's homely side revealed alongside the usual quick-draw sharpshooting.

Wayne accepts his Best Actor Academy
Award for *True Grit* from Barbra
Streisand, April 7, 1970.

Celebrating a Golden Globe Awards win with actress Ann-Margret, 1970.

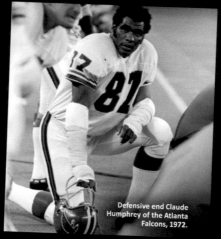
Defensive end Claude Humphrey of the Atlanta Falcons, 1972.

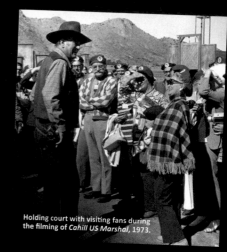
Holding court with visiting fans during the filming of *Cahill US Marshal*, 1973.

A MAJOR BLOW CAME WITH THE DEATH OF JOHN FORD IN 1973.

In 1972, Wayne received an unusual but highly treasured honor when the Atlanta Falcons selected him as a player, even though he was then 64 years old. Although the draft into the NFL was likely a publicity stunt, as Wayne knew perfectly well, it was still a historic moment—eventhough the humorless football league made it clear that he would not be permitted to play.

Sadly for Wayne, his strength was ebbing by this point, and a major blow came with the death of John Ford in the summer of 1973. The cinema establishment had known that "Pappy" was on his way out for some time, having honored him with the American Film Institute's Lifetime Achievement Award in March that year. Even the White House stepped up, with President Nixon promoting Ford—a World War II veteran—to Admiral and giving him the Presidential Medal of Freedom.

When Ford died, it was a serious blow to Wayne, who was promoting Andrew V. McLaglen's *Cahill U.S. Marshal* at the time. Now suffering from emphysema in his one remaining lung, the other one having been removed back in 1964, he was finding the burden of filming action roles a little too much, even using a stepladder to mount a horse on set. He famously told a posse of reporters, "I'm pretty much living on borrowed time."

The question for Wayne, then, was what to do with the years he had left. One thing was for sure: he wasn't planning to go quietly.

GIVE 'EM HELL, JOHN.

John Wayne in
A Howard Hawks Production
"Rio Lobo"
A Cinema Center Films Presentation

BELGA FILMS presente
JOHN WAYNE ~ RICHARD BOONE
BIG JAKE
A CINEMA CENTER FILMS PRESENTATION
PATRICK WAYNE ~ CHRISTOPHER MITCHUM
MAUREEN O'HARA
UN FILM DE GEORGE SHERMAN
SCOPE-COULEUR

Wayne with his longtime mentor John Ford, 1971.

THE PLAYBOY INTERVIEW

Wayne was nothing if not candid, but the views he aired in a
1971 interview shocked America.

By JOEL MCIVER

A ny modern discussion of John
Wayne should include a mention
of an interview that he gave
to *Playboy* in 1971, because it
reveals pretty much everything
about his worldview at the
time. Few people have read it,
because it's 12,000 words long and not particularly
easy to find, but there are transcripts on the
internet.

Wayne's interviewer was *Playboy*'s Contributing
Editor Richard Warren Lewis, who was
surprisingly but admirably combative with his
questions: such an approach with an equivalent
movie star today would certainly be blocked by
the celeb's handlers. The interview took place on
Wayne's yacht, Wild Goose. A second meeting
took place a week later at Batjac's production
offices, and Lewis stitched it all together to
produce the final piece.

Looking back, Lewis wrote, "Wayne greeted
me on a manicured lawn against a backdrop

of sailboats, motor cruisers, and yachts plying
Newport Harbor. Wearing a realistic toupee,
Wayne at first appeared considerably younger
than he is; only the liver spots on both hands and
the lines in his jut-jawed face told of his 63 years.
But at 6 foot 4 inches and 244 pounds, it still
almost seems as if he could have single-handedly
mopped up all those bad guys from the Panhandle
to Guadalcanal."

At the 1971 Grammy Awards, where he presented a Grammy to Paul McCartney.

Rinsing off on the set of *Big Jake*, 1971.

Over a "high-protein diet lunch of char-broiled steak, lettuce, and cottage cheese" and a few shots of tequila, Lewis asked Wayne about a range of subjects, including the state of the movie business ("I'm glad I won't be around much longer to see what they do with it," said Wayne), sex in film ("When you think of the wonderful picture fare we've had through the years and realize we've come to this . . . it's disgusting"), and violence on screen. ("Pictures go too far when they use that kind of realism, when they have shots of blood spurting out and teeth flying, and when they throw liver out to make it look like people's insides.")

In 1999, Wayne's gravestone was amended with a profound quote that read, "Tomorrow is the most important thing. Comes into us at midnight very clean. It's perfect when it arrives and it puts itself in our hands. It hopes we've learned something from yesterday." This thought-provoking point came from *Playboy*: in other words, Wayne's final statement came from his most controversial interview.

Delivering a telling punch in *Big Jake*, 1971.

Wayne appearing on NBC sketch comedy shown *Rowan and Martin's Laugh-In*, 1971.

SMALL-SCREEN

Wayne wasn't just a big-screen star—TV
beamed him into homes across America.

★ ★ ★ ★ ★

By JOEL McIVER

Wayne and Red Skelton on *The Red Skelton Show.*

STAR

Filming the intro to *Gunsmoke* in 1955.

Talk show host Michael Parkinson interviews Wayne, January 1974.

 [HE WAS VISIBLE ON TV] IN TALK SHOWS, DOCUMENTARIES, AND COMMERCIALS.

"I don't know if I love it or hate it," said John Wayne when asked what he thought about television in 1972, "but there sure has never been any form of entertainment so available to the human race with so little effort since they invented marital sex."

This pithy quote reveals pretty clearly what the Duke thought about the small screen, at least as it was in the early seventies. Back then, as anyone over 40 will remember, TV was very much the lesser sibling of the movie experience, populated—in America anyway—by spineless soap operas replete with advertising. Unlike today's all-powerful televisual medium, which effortlessly overpowers the draw of cinema, seventies TV was where actors went after their careers had begun to plateau—or fade away.

Wayne never had to take the TV-actor route, because his film career only ran out of steam when he himself did. The closest he came was a rumored offer to star in the radio-show-turned-TV-production *Gunsmoke* in 1955: rather than take the part, he filmed an introduction to the pilot episode.

Still, he dipped in and out of the occasional television drama, with a cameo role here and a pilot episode there. Where he was visible on TV was in talk shows, documentaries, awards ceremonies, and commercials, all of which served his career in different, lucrative ways.

The first category, the celebrity talk show, was always a popular draw for Wayne, and he regularly returned to many of these. Across his career he appeared no fewer than 15 times on *Rowan & Martin's Laugh-In*, 10 times on *The Merv Griffin Show*, on six occasions each with Bob Hope and Johnny Carson, four with Dean Martin, three each with Red Skelton and Ed Sullivan, and twice with Joey Bishop and Milton Berle. He also appeared on two versions of *This is Your Life*, one of them the Australian variant. In the UK, he was interviewed on TV by David Frost and Michael Parkinson.

Wayne also donated his time to appearing in campaign ads for the presidential hopefuls Barry Goldwater (1964) and Richard Nixon (1968), as well as for Ronald Reagan's California Governor bid in 1966. He promoted the US Marine Corps on screen twice and did the same for various charitable causes, as well as banking a sizeable check for ads for Camel cigarettes, Old Gold Filters, and Gillette razors.

In the YouTube era, Wayne fans can access no end of TV highlights, from the good to the bad to the unutterably cheesy. Check out his guest spot on Raquel Welch's TV special, *Raquel!*, from April 26, 1970, in which he gives his hostess lessons in gunfighting, all shot on a Western backlot interspersed with clips from his films.

On November 29 the same year, Wayne appeared in an NBC special sponsored by Budweiser called *Swing Out, Sweet Land*, a patriotic documentary about the US. Apparently 30 million American homes tuned into the 90-minute show, which also featured Red Skelton, Lorne Greene, Dean Martin, and Bob Hope.

In fact, documentaries turned out to be a decent vehicle for Wayne, who could ally his personal values with the subject at hand and do a convincing job. Take a look at *Harry Jackson: A Man and His Art* and *The American West of John Ford*, devoted respectively to the renowned sculptor and director. Wayne also appeared in *Directed by John Ford*, the American Film Institute's 1971 tribute to his filmic mentor, narrated by Orson Welles and directed by the legendary Peter Bogdanovich.

You'll also find Wayne appearing on *The Glen Campbell Show* in 1971, touring the John Wayne Theater at Knotts Berry Farm; meeting Campbell again three years later on *The Musical West*, an NBC special; battling it out in 1974 with the liberal host on *Maude Meets the Duke*; and surprising the normally savage comedian Don Rickles on a 1975 *Bob Hope* special by walking out on stage unannounced.

Perhaps oddly given the Duke's profile, he did quite a bit of TV comedy as well, often playing the role of the straight guy to the clownish presenter. He appeared on *The Super Comedy Bowl* in 1971, hosted by Lucille Ball, and on *Everything You Always Wanted to Know About Jack Benny but were Afraid to Ask* with Ball again and George Burns.

Remarkably, Wayne was actually talked into putting on a sky-blue bunny suit (below right) for the 1972 season opener of *Laugh-In*, filming short cameos that the show used over the next year.

Lucille Ball and Wayne in *The Lucy Show.*

Wayne appearing on *The Dean Martin Show.*

Bea Arthur and Wayne perform in *Maude Meets the Duke*, 1974.

END CREDITS

In 1979, Wayne confronted his final call with the courage that had defined his life.

By JOEL McIVER

In 1973 John Wayne was 67 years old. Realizing that the clock was ticking, Wayne signed up for a film called *McQ*, in which he played a police detective threatened by a professional hitman.

Three years before, Wayne had been denied the starring role in *Dirty Harry*. The part went to the much younger Clint Eastwood, making him a huge star as the archetype for badass cops who don't play by the rules but get the job done anyway. Clearly regretting this decision, Wayne went for *McQ* instead, but by then the moment had passed and it was only a moderate success.

Another policeman role followed for Wayne in 1975, this time in *Brannigan*, but this time it was set and shot in London at a time in English history when Britain should really have been called Grey rather than Great. In these unlikely environs for

cinema's favorite cowboy, Wayne's Chicago police lieutenant Jim Brannigan is tasked with retrieving an American mafioso. His methods are, shall we say, a little more extreme than those employed by the unarmed English bobbies of the day, and in the end he gets his man in the bloody manner to which we have become accustomed.

"*Brannigan* isn't great, but it's a well-crafted action movie and besides, it's got John Wayne in it," noted critic Roger Ebert.

Much more appealing to the American public was 1975's *Rooster Cogburn*, a heartwarming spinoff from *True Grit*, the 1969 Western in which Wayne had played the Falstaffian title character to much acclaim. Alongside Katharine Hepburn as his leading lady, Wayne came as close as he'd ever come to hamming it up on screen in a story that sees him chasing down a band of bank robbers. The two stars, just two weeks apart in age, both stayed in Sunriver, Oregon, near the shoot: they even entertained a visit from the state's Governor Tom McCall.

By 1976, Wayne was in poor shape, although not yet actually ill, but he had the time and the energy for one more film role. Fortunately, it turned out to be a beauty: the part of sheriff-turned-gunfighter John Bernard "J.B." Books in *The Shootist* alongside Lauren Bacall, the young Ron Howard, and James Stewart.

Paul Newman had rejected this role, as had George C. Scott, Charles Bronson, Gene Hackman, and Clint Eastwood: Wayne had not been considered because he was known to be seriously unfit. Once he had secured the part, though, he made it through the shoot more or less unscathed, although the high altitude of the Nevada location exhausted him and he needed to take a week off to recover from the flu.

It's easy to understand why the critics liked *The Shootist*. Wayne does a charismatic job of carrying the film, but he isn't the swashbuckling alpha male of before: instead, Books' health is failing and he receives a terminal cancer diagnosis. Unwilling to accept a peaceful death, he arranges to fight three men known for their violent reputations in a bar. While he manages to dispatch the trio, the bartender shoots him in the back: he dies happy.

Although the director was Don Siegel, the movie was essentially owned by Wayne, who influenced its screenplay and casting simply through being too hardheaded to compromise.

Not coincidentally, the movie's plot overlaps quite a lot with that of *The Gunfighter* (1950), whose starring role Wayne had wanted but rejected because he hated the studio head Harry Cohn.

As Wayne's contract gave him approval over the script, he changed the entire nature of the movie. First he moved the location from El Paso to Carson City; then he removed a scene where he is required to shoot someone in the back,

John Wayne in *McQ*, 1974.

With Katharine Hepburn in *Rooster Cogburn*.

BIG JIM BRANNIGAN TAKES ON LONDON – *CHICAGO STYLE!*

JOHN WAYNE IS "BRANNIGAN!"

Pitching during a charity baseball game, April 1977.

(From left to right) Peter Fonda, Wayne, and Henry Fonda at the Beverly Hilton Hotel in Beverly Hills.

"A GALLBLADDER PROCEDURE ... REVEALED THAT HE WAS SUFFERING FROM STOMACH CANCER.

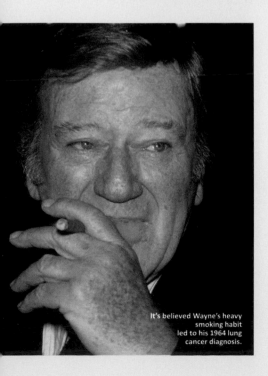

It's believed Wayne's heavy smoking habit led to his 1964 lung cancer diagnosis.

which he refused to do on grounds of gentlemanly honor; and he also rewrote the bartender as Books' killer. Then he arranged for his friends Bacall, Stewart, and others to be cast and enjoyed a fine old time with them on set. In one scene, he and Stewart got their lines wrong so many times that Siegel begged them to try harder. "If you want the scene done better," chuckled Wayne, "you'd better get yourself a couple of better actors."

The industry appreciated all this, with the National Board of Review naming *The Shootist* one of the 10 Best Films of 1976. The film was also nominated for an Oscar, a Golden Globe, a BAFTA award, and a Writers' Guild of America award.

Too little, too late, perhaps? It's probable that Wayne didn't care: he had bigger concerns on his mind. In 1978 he underwent open-heart surgery to

replace a defective valve. Afterwards, he said, "I guess I'm just too goddamned tough to die," but he spoke too soon, as a gallbladder procedure in January the following year revealed that he was suffering from stomach cancer.

Wayne's son Patrick told the press at the time that the doctors had been surprised to find the cancer but that his father was not. "He had been complaining for quite a while," he said. "His internist thought it was stress, but my dad kept saying, 'I have cancer. I've had cancer before, and I know how it feels, and I have it now.'"

Images Getty Images, Alamy

105

Promoting the ABC TV special *General Electric's All-Star Anniversary* with Elizabeth Taylor.

Wayne with his two youngest daughters, Aissa (left) and Marisa.

THE END

❝ IT SOON BECAME APPARENT THAT WAYNE'S CANCER WAS INCURABLE.

"But when they tested him, they couldn't find anything. So everyone thought he was crazy. And by the time he had the gallbladder surgery, it was pretty advanced. His doctors removed as much of his stomach as possible, and also the lymph system, but because the cancer was so far advanced, the surgery wasn't effective."

Stomach cancer is still difficult to cure today, but in the seventies it was even more serious. It's thought nowadays that the decline in the disease since then is partly attributable to most people's increased intake of fresh fruit and vegetables, as well as improvements in methods of preserving food. This was not fully understood back in 1979, though, and when Wayne heard about an experimental cancer research group at UCLA led by an oncologist called Donald Morton, he signed up.

It was soon apparent that Wayne's cancer was incurable, though, and the establishment took the opportunity to make a gesture of recognition before it was too late. The government awarded him the Congressional Gold Medal on his 72nd birthday on May 26, with stars including Maureen O'Hara, Elizabeth Taylor, Frank Sinatra, Katharine Hepburn, Gregory Peck, and Kirk Douglas paying tribute at the ceremony.

Robert Aldrich, the president of the Directors Guild of America, stated, "I am a registered Democrat, and to my knowledge, share none of the political views espoused by Duke. However, whether he is ill disposed or healthy, John Wayne is far beyond the normal political sharpshooting in this community. Because of his courage, his dignity, his integrity, and because of his talents as an actor, his strength as a leader, his

warmth as a human being throughout his illustrious career, he is entitled to a unique spot in our hearts and minds."

At the Oscar's ceremony on April 9, 1979, Wayne—gaunt, pale, and breathless—receives a standing ovation before presenting the Best Picture award. Although he bravely promises, "I plan to be around for a long time yet," the exhaustion in his face and voice indicate otherwise. It was his last public appearance. Just six weeks later, on June 11, one of Hollywood's

most iconic tough guys died, his body finally surrendering to a disease he'd fought valiantly.

"I didn't think he'd die," said Patrick Wayne. "I thought he'd beat this like he did in 1964. He never seemed to give up. And though he was in tremendous pain, he never gave in to it, and he never let it get to him. When I look back on it now, I realize that the reason he was demonstrating that courage was that he needed to do that for his family."

A visibly ailing Wayne waves to the audience at the 1979 Academy Awards.

Images Getty Images, Alamy

WAYNE'S WORLD

Hollywood's most iconic tough guy didn't just grace cinema—he changed it.

By NEIL CROSSLEY

 n a career spanning over half a century and 169 films, John Wayne dominated movie screens and rose through the ranks to become one of the most popular film stars in cinema history.

As his fame grew, he evolved from an actor to an all-American icon, his no-nonsense persona and strict moral code embodying everything that many felt was great and good about America.

In some ways, Wayne's persona was carefully calculated. Meeting Wyatt Earp on the set of a John Ford Western in 1928 left a lasting impression on him. Wayne acknowledged that his trademark swagger and laconic drawl were fashioned on Earp. Wayne became

 WAYNE TRANSFORMED FIGHT SCENES, ENSURING THAT THEY LOOKED MUCH MORE CONVINCING.

synonymous with Westerns, but in the post-war years also rose to become the quintessential hero in a succession of war films.

One of Wayne's greatest contributions to cinema is the realism that he brought to the Western genre. Along with renowned stuntman Yakima Canutt, Wayne transformed fight scenes, ensuring that they looked much more convincing. "Before I came along, it was standard practice that the hero must always fight clean," he said.

By the mid 1950s, alongside younger actors such as Marlon Brando, Wayne's depictions became rooted in much

greater realism. It's a shift that can be viewed in what is arguably his finest work, John Ford's 1956 Western *The Searchers*.

"I think John Wayne in *The Searchers* is the greatest performance in the history of cinema," said esteemed film historian John Milius. It's a view that was echoed by critic John Powers of National Public Radio (NPR) in 2011: "Even in routine pictures, he dominated the screen as few stars ever have, often by appearing to do nothing. A master of silence, he knew the camera, was the best reactor this side of Cary Grant, and didn't fear emotion."

Some have argued that Wayne simply played himself, but many esteemed critics argue that this view misses the depth of his talent. Wayne had a capacity to convey quiet tenderness in his roles and was capable of finely nuanced portrayals of complex characters.

Sadly, Wayne's legacy has remained controversial especially in light of the prejudiced comments he made in that infamous *Playboy* interview. Some find it difficult to separate the man from his art, but as an actor, his reputation is up there with the finest.

"Wayne was a hell of an actor," recalled Robert Duvall. "He understood his characters inherently and knew exactly what the director needed from him. He understood everything about cameras and lenses, but it all started with him. He did what all great actors do, he strived for the truth." Above all else, that is the most vital thing an actor can do.

Images Getty Images, Alamy

JOHN WAYNE
BY NUMBERS

142

Amount of times Wayne held the leading role in a film, a record figure

179

FEATURE FILMS & TV SHOWS

1 **ACADEMY AWARD WIN**
TRUE GRIT, 1969 & 3 NOMINATIONS

1 **GRAMMY NOMINATION**
"AMERICA, WHY I LOVE HER," 1972

ESTIMATED TICKET SALES UP TO THE YEAR 2000

$1.1 BILLION

$700 million
US BOX-OFFICE TAKINGS FROM HIS FILMS

HOW THE WEST WAS WON

23 MILLION

WAS WAYNE'S HIGHEST-GROSSING FILM

13 lbs

Weight at birth

3 MARRIAGES

$7 MILLION NET WORTH
at time of his death